PRAISE FOR
BADASS MANIFESTING

"Jenny Block has taken manifesting from the 'woo woo' world to the real world with this charming guide that helps badasses—and those soon to be badasses—find, free, and be their very best selves."

—**Noah Michelson**, director of *HuffPost Personal* and cohost of the famed HuffPost podcast *Am I Doing It Wrong*

"The world needs a guide to the subject of being a badass, and I can't think of a better person to supply it than Jenny. She definitely knows a thing or two about power, domination, style, and an overall take-no-prisoners outlook that we all can learn from."

—**Isaac Mizrahi**, performer and internationally known fashion designer

"Jenny offers a fun, digestible, and perspective-driven reminder—via memorable mantras, relatable expositions, and her signature positive spirit—that we don't need permission from anyone to live a Life of Yes."

—**Sara K. Runnels**, writer and humorist

"No one does it better than Jenny! We should all learn how to better advocate for ourselves, and this book shows you how to do that in true badass style. It opens up a world of possibilities! It shows you how positive thought outweighs negative, helping you to achieve your dreams."

—**Nicole Miller**, fashion designer

"Badass Manifesting is my kind of book—no-nonsense, in-your-face, and straightforward. I detest empty clichés that promise magic results, and this book has none of that dribble-drabble. These are the kinds of manifestations that I believe truly work. Jenny Block has put them in one convenient place and delivers them in small, bite-sized, easily digestible pieces. This book has such an open-minded perspective; whatever your belief system is, you will feel seen and invited to participate. I believe in *active* meditation and the ability to sculpt *your* life, starting with that little voice in your head. Jenny arms that voice with the right words to motivate change and manifest dreams...like the badasses we all truly are."

—**Christina Wells**, AGT semifinalist, Broadway national touring artist, and motivational speaker

BADASS MANIFESTING

BOOKS BY THE AUTHOR

Be That Unicorn. Find Your Magic. Live Your Truth. Share Your Shine (2020)

The Ultimate Guide to Solo Sex (2016)

O Wow: Discovering Your Ultimate Orgasm (2015)

Open: Love, Sex, and Life in an Open Marriage (2008)

BADASS MANIFESTING

HOW TO MANIFEST ABUNDANCE, SUCCESS, AND THE JOYFUL LIFE OF YOUR DREAMS

by JENNY BLOCK

Books That Save Lives

Published by BTSL/Jim Dandy Publishing
6252 Peach Avenue
Van Nuys, CA 91411
info@jimdandypublishing.com

For bulk orders, special quantities, course adoptions, and corporate sales,
please email info@jimdandypublishing.com

ISBN: (print) 978-1-68481-748-1, (ebook) 978-1-68481-749-8
BISAC: SEL004000, SELF-HELP / Affirmations

Printed in the United States of America

For my daughter, Hannah, a true badass.

"Be scared and f**king do it anyway!"

—Desiree Asher

"Manifesting, for me, is listening to the whisper of who you truly are—and choosing, every day, to water that voice until it blooms."

—Plant Kween (Christopher Griffin),
Author, Educator, Creator

Table of Contents

Foreword *by Rabbi Kenneth Block (a.k.a. my dad)* 14

INTRODUCTION: You Are Already a Badass. Now Let's Manifest the Life You Long For 16

How to Use This Book 29

Like a Badass, of Course!

CHAPTER ONE: You Hold the Secret to Manifesting Your Desires 35

If You Are Willing to Ask for Anything, You Just Might Find Yourself Getting Everything

CHAPTER TWO: The Only Permission You Need to Manifest Your Dreams Comes from You 49

If You Are the One to Give Yourself Permission, You Will Always Have Permission

CHAPTER THREE: It's Okay to Question Your Journey Because You Know the Answers 62

If I Can Ask the Question, I Can Find the Answer

CHAPTER FOUR: You Know Your Badass Self and You Have No Reason to Hide It 76

If You Know Who You Are, No One Can Take That Away from You

CHAPTER FIVE: When You Lift Others Up, You Lift Yourself Up Too 89

If You Can Support Someone Else in Their Journey, You Will Find Yourself Supported as Well

**CHAPTER SIX: You Have a Right to Everything You
Are and Everything You Have** 102

*When I Achieve Something, It's Because I Deserve
to Achieve It*

**CHAPTER SEVEN: You Get to Decide What the
Badass Version of You Looks Like** 116

*If You Are Comfortable in Your Own Skin, You Will
Always Find Comfort*

**CHAPTER EIGHT: You Get to Start Fresh Every
Day and Leave the Past Where It Belongs** 130

*If You Can Let Yesterday Go, You Can Take Advantage
of All of Today's Possibilities*

**CHAPTER NINE: You Are Not Alone in Your
Manifesting Journey** 142

If You Can Trust in the Universe, You Can Trust Yourself

**CHAPTER TEN: You Can Handle Whatever
Comes Your Way** 155

If You Can Handle the Worst, You'll Be Ready for the Best

**CHAPTER ELEVEN: You Can Open Yourself to Others
and Expand Your Manifesting Powers** 168

*If You Can Let Others In, You Can Find Your Way in
the World*

**CHAPTER TWELVE: You Can Take a Chance on
Yourself and Trust Your Choices** 181

*If You Can Take a Chance on Yourself, You'll Give
Yourself More than Just a Chance*

**CHAPTER THIRTEEN: You Can Say No Without
Feeling Guilty to Protect Your Badassery** 193

*If You Sometimes Say No to Others, You Can Always
Say Yes to Yourself*

**CHAPTER FOURTEEN: You Can Handle
Compliments and Complaints with Ease** 205

If You Can Absorb the Love, You Can Deflect the Hate

**CHAPTER FIFTEEN: You Know Your Story and
You Can Trust What It Teaches You** 218

If You Can Keep Looking Within, You'll Never Feel Without

**CONCLUSION: You Don't Just Have the Magic,
You Are the Magic. Now Let's Make Some Magic!** 232

   Story Storage 235

   Mantra Manufacturing 240

   Takeaway Treasure Chest 245

   Compliment Cabinet 250

   Complaint Compartment 254

   Processing Pages 258

Acknowledgments 263

About the Author 265

FOREWORD
by Rabbi Kenneth Block
(a.k.a. my dad)

Manifesting has for too long been thought to be about visualizing something in your mind that you want and hoping it will magically happen. Manifesting has become about practices like repeating positive phrases and surrounding yourself with posters to help you imagine achieving something. It has become the belief that just wishing, picturing, hoping, and praying will make it happen. People's beliefs about manifesting have come to be based on the idea that you can think your dreams into reality without actually doing any of the work that is required to reach your goals.

We used to call it wishful thinking, or magical thinking.

You can manifest what you want in life or who you want to be—but only by connecting your thinking with concrete, positive actions that can lead to your goal. Start by focusing on what you want. Then do what will make it happen.

The journey to your goal starts from where you are. A good map and a compass are necessities for any journey. This book is both a map and a compass. Use the map to manifest the route you will take to get to your goal. Use the compass to guide your steps and your actions.

You are not going to "try" to manifest, you are going to manifest. Spread your map out in front of you; see where you are; and visualize the journey to your goal. Look at the route; picture your destination, the places you will visit on the way, and where you will stop and rest; and then see yourself arriving at your goal. Now, take out your compass, place it in the palm of your hand, and start doing what needs to be done: Manifesting—thinking, visualizing, dreaming, and *doing*, truly taking action—and make the journey.

As Rabbi Hillel once said, "If not now...when?"

INTRODUCTION

YOU ARE ALREADY A BADASS. NOW LET'S MANIFEST THE LIFE YOU LONG FOR

We all have a badass inside of us, someone who stands up for themselves and others; someone who gets shit done; someone who knows what they want and makes it happen and doesn't let anyone—or anything—stand in their way.

The trouble is, sometimes that badass is a little too deep inside of us and struggles to get out. Fear all too often keeps us from being our true badass selves. Depression and anxiety can make that actualization tough too.

This book will help you manifest the badass you truly are so you can live the badass life you truly deserve to live. So, buckle up and let the badassery begin!

I'm guessing that if you want to be a badass, you probably already are. You just need to manifest your badass self. Maybe you don't know how. Maybe you're afraid it's a bad thing. Maybe you don't trust that you really *are* a badass. Well, you can let all of that go. It's time to manifest. Why?

Well, for starters, being a badass is a good thing, a really good thing on all counts. Think about the badasses you know. Family, friends, colleagues, celebs—people making things happen in a way that, from the outside, looks downright magical.

Well, it's also you. Or it can be, anyway. All you need to do is let your inner badass out. And this just might be the most revealing, most inspiring, most interesting journey you will ever take.

I like the word badassery. I didn't invent it, but I sure would like to cement its place in the modern lexicon. I like it because it sounds like wizardry or sorcery, except it's real, and I can prove it. Well, actually, you can prove it. Not to me: You don't have to prove it to me, or to anyone else for that matter. That's the other great thing about badassery. The only person you have to prove it to is yourself, and *voila!*—you are then a badass, which entitles you to all the privileges of badassery.

Now what?

I imagine that's what you're thinking. How do I become this badass? Or rather, how do I let out my inner badass? Well, you manifest it. I know; that sounds like one of those sayings on a sign or a coffee mug you might pick up at one of those annoyingly cute little boutiques. I mean, it sounds nice, but how on Earth can I do that? *Can* I even do that? I mean maybe some people can, but probably not me. Well, I have a little story about that to share with you.

I have always been a little leery about manifesting. I mean, how could that possibly work? I'm just one person—just me. There's a whole universe out there. Isn't it like using a Ouija board? I mean, finding things out with a Ouija board could be a cool idea. But someone is pushing it, right? Well, right. Someone or something is pushing it, even if not consciously, because here's the thing: it's all energy; life is all energy; we're all energy. So, we can use that energy to spell out words on a board, and we can use it to charge ourselves up and open ourselves up to the outcomes we desire.

Now, manifestation is not a vending machine. And you can't fight the laws of physics—most of us can't, anyway. But we *can* set ourselves up for success. That's what manifesting is really about: bringing forth the best version of you to create the best possible life for yourself.

And every once in a while, it does seem to work like magic. And that's where the little story I mentioned comes in. I was working at a music festival in Michigan called Fern Fest, which, in its first year, took place in a location lovingly referred to simply as "The Land." It's where the Michigan Womyn's Music Festival took place for forty years.

Anyway, to make a long story at least a little shorter, there are ongoing fundraising efforts by the We Want the Land Coalition to ensure that The Land always remains "For Women. For Girls. Forever," which it now is, the way. So the summer I was there, they were doing a fifty/fifty raffle. You buy a ticket and, if you win, you get half the proceeds and "The Land" gets the other half. I told my friend Mollie, "I need to win—so I can give them my half too." She said, "Let's manifest it." I figured I had nothing to lose, so I said, "Show me the way."

Mollie is a practitioner of the traditional Chinese energy technique of *qigong*, which is where she learned her manifesting practice. We did some movement exercises to center ourselves, and then she said, "I want you to picture yourself winning. Where are you? What does that sound like? How does that feel in your body? I want you to imagine yourself telling someone that you won. Where are you? What does that sound like? How does that feel? Don't just imagine it, *be* there. Be there in that moment of winning."

So I did. I did that in the moment, and I did it over and over, and on Friday, as we sat under the tent awaiting the final show, I heard, "And the winner of the fifty/fifty drawing is...Jenny Block."

I could hardly believe it. That was four years ago, and I can still hardly believe it. Did we change the particles in the air? Was it a magic trick? Would I have won without the careful movement, the mindful breathing, and the intentional thinking? I don't know. We can't ever know.

What I do know is that I won and I felt incredibly powerful for having won. And in that moment, I knew anything was possible. Not everything— but anything.

To be fair, I used the same practice again when applying to the MFA program at NYU, and after two tries, I still have not gotten in yet. But that's not because it doesn't work or because I didn't do it well enough or hard enough. It just wasn't to be. And so it wasn't. Not in that moment, anyway. Who knows what came to me instead because I didn't get what I thought I wanted? Maybe it wasn't the right time. Maybe it wasn't the right thing. Maybe it wasn't the right way.

Manifesting is about bringing forth what is meant to be. It helps you to not miss what the universe has waiting for you. It does not create out of thin air what was not meant for you.

But you have to believe it. You have to believe, not in some sort of "woo woo" magic, but in yourself, and in your ability to be your best self, and in your ability to create and be open to the opportunities that are meant for you. There are plenty of things in life set to thwart us—from natural disasters to evil people. There are plenty of constraints we have to work within, like the physical reality we learn about from science and sharing this planet with other creatures and beings. We can't control everything. But we can control ourselves and how we interface with the world around us.

And we cannot ignore that there is a world around us, which is why one of the toughest things about manifesting is the focus it requires. You say your mantra, and then your phone dings or your alarm reminds you that you have a meeting in ten minutes or your spouse or kid or pet demands attention. Life is a lot. Even if you have your basic needs met, it's a lot. All the more so if you don't.

Manifesting takes time. And it takes brain space, which can be even harder to come by. So I have done my very best to assure that this book will help you on your journey even with these challenges. For one, each mantra comes with five questions. You say the mantra. You answer the question. And then you repeat the process. By the time you you finish the process, your brain and your focus will be locked in on the target.

I don't mean to be morbid, but if (God forbid) you had cancer, you'd "find time" for treatment, right? Well, I'm asking you to save yourself from missing out on the life that is meant for you. Who do you want to be today? If the answer is your badass self, great! This book will set you on the path to manifesting exactly that. If not, this book will help you find out why that is and hopefully get you on track to wanting the badass best for yourself.

Too many of us, especially women, feel like we don't deserve time to ourselves. There's an old and not so funny saying about moms on vacation that goes something like "Same activities, different view." This is because even on vacation, women often find themselves caretaking and tidying as well as carrying the mental load of logistics and planning for the family, plus coping with the age-old question, "What's for dinner?"

But here's the thing: You do deserve time for yourself, and if you don't take it, you will at some point hit a wall of sadness, resentment, or just plain "over-it-ness." (That may not be a word. But it certainly should be.)

You get to choose. All day, every day, you get to choose. You get to make so many little choices that all add up to your life: what you eat; how you move your body; who you spend your time with. That's what manifesting is really about—building the life you want by making choices that support that life. You can't have everything, and very little is instant. But you can have a lot; and a year from now, it will be a year from now, and it's totally up to you whether you're closer to who you want to be or not.

Manifesting is not a magic trick, it's a state of mindfulness. It's a misnomer that you can manifest money or a job or any specific outcome or object. What you can manifest is a daily commitment to be your best in order to achieve your best with the tools you have. When my dad used to teach a general religious studies class at my high school, he would start on the first day by coming into the classroom and saying, "Okay, God. Prove to me you're real. Present before me a red bicycle." Then he would stand back and wait. "God? Are you there? Where's the bicycle?" Then he would wait again.

As the students tittered in their seats, he would gather his things and start to walk out.

The students would ask where he was going, and
he would say, "I'm leaving. There's no point in
having this class if there's no God...right?" But the
students would protest and tell him, "That's not how
God works!"

"Right!" my father would say. "God helps those who
help themselves. God doesn't make bicycles appear.
He makes us smart, kind, resourceful, strong people
who can create ways to have the lives we desire,
including lives with bicycles."

Manifesting is just like that. It's not about magic, it's
about faith. Some people trust in God or the universe
or humankind or themselves or any combination
thereof. The manifestations of that faith are your
dreams becoming reality.

People tend to give up when their wishes aren't
granted. But this isn't *Aladdin*. This is real life. And
manifesting only works if you *work it.*

This book and the mantras you'll be exploring in
later sections are about finding out what makes you
a badass, not about trying to make you someone
you're not. That would be pointless. But if you
can find your own individual superpower and then
respect and grow it, you can basically do anything.

How do you think Taylor Swift became a superstar after playing to less than a dozen people at a hot dog festival? How did Lady Gaga manage to persevere after she learned of the "I hate Stephanie" club? How did they keep the faith? How did they trust themselves and the universe? How did they stand firm in their badassery?

They watched for the glimmers, and on your badass journey, you will learn to do the same. Glimmers are the tiny things—or not so tiny things—that help to remind you that you are a badass even when it feels like you're not. It's getting the regular height table at the restaurant for your friend with the double hip replacements when they only had bar height tables with tall stools available. It's speaking Spanish with the elderly woman on the flight who's alone and scared and doesn't speak any English. It's getting to headline a comedy show for the very first time. It's things you made happen because you're you. And if you can do those little things, just imagine the big things you can do.

The mantras in this book will reaffirm who you are and what you can do. They are different from others you may have encountered because they aren't hollow. They didn't appear out of the ether, they came out of my own life and out of my own cautionary tales, out of the times when at first I didn't listen to my inner badass and what happened when I finally did.

Our missteps are actually just steps along our path through life if we choose to use them that way. But we have to choose them and use them instead of dismissing them.

Here's the thing, all too many self-help books are all ribbons and roses. I don't know about you, but my life is certainly not all ribbons and roses. These books make me feel like a failure before I even start. "Stop worrying!" they scream. "Just focus!" they demand. "Life is easy if you just do it right!"

"I wish I could!" "Why didn't I think of that?" "What the heck is right?" I want to scream back at those well-meaning "experts."

The truth is, I've always had trouble with the mantra thing. I mean, if I'm looking into the mirror every day and saying, "I'm good enough, I'm smart enough, and doggone it, people like me," what's that going to accomplish that makes a difference to my life?

This is the mantra book for anyone and everyone. You don't have to be anyone other than yourself in order to be everything you want to be. That's because this is a book about manifesting from the ashes, about taking all of the things that happened to you—both the good and the bad—and using them to show yourself how incredible you are. Because it's time you stopped ignoring that fact.

I am a badass. I manifested the badass life I have. And I so often encounter people who aren't sure how to trust themselves. Well, this is how. If it feels impossible, it's because you just haven't worked out how to make it happen...yet. Allow me to be your guide.

Think of my stories as fables or even fairy tales, sometimes the Brothers Grimm kind. The only difference is that these stories are mine and they are true, and like a good badass, I want to share them and what I learned from them. Gatekeeping is simply not in my nature.

As I was thinking about writing this book, I thought a lot about where mantras emanate from and why we should bother to take on or buy into certain ones and eschew others. The answer I came up with is that the mantras that work are the ones that come from something real and experienced and universally true. Although you may not have experienced the exact same thing I've experienced, you likely did or could have or would have, but by the grace of the universe you have lived your life and I have lived mine.

Here's what I want you know above all else, even if you don't read another page of this book:

You can have the power of manifesting. You in fact have the power of manifesting. The truth is, you *are* the power of manifesting. I'm just here to help you unleash and harness that power. That's exactly what each chapter and each mantra will do. You want to be a badass? You want to live a badass life? And do badass things? Okay then!

Let's get to some badass manifesting. I'll start.

My name is Jenny Block.
I am a badass.

HOW TO USE THIS BOOK
Like a Badass, of Course!

Here's the drill. If you can, do this first thing in the morning when you are alone, and do it out loud. If the only option is in your head in the carpool lane or on the subway or at your desk at the office, that's okay too! Better somewhere than nowhere!

For each chapter's mantra:

Say the mantra in your head. Then repeat the mantra out loud. Ask yourself the question and answer it in your head. Do that until you work through all of the questions. End by reciting the mantra once more in your head and then once more out loud. Then, write the mantra down somewhere. You can keep a little notepad or journal nearby or even use a notes app on your phone. At some later point, share the mantra—maybe tell your partner, your friend, or your mom. That last step can really energize you to make it real.

You can read the chapter straightaway or wait until later in the day, but do your best to start with the mantra each day.

For extra credit, repeat the mantra-and-question process once more before bed. At the very least, say the mantra to yourself as many times as you like as you fall asleep. This method has the added benefit of keeping your brain from overthinking, and instead, gives your mind something positive to chew on.

You can do a mantra per day or per week or per month. You can combine them as you go through and try different mantras. You can say certain sets you choose, or all of them if you like. This book is about finding your way. My job is to give you enough tools to at least start your journey and hopefully plenty to keep you going, including helping you to create mantras all your own.

At the end of this book, you will find a series of tools. Each one has an explanation of how to use the tool, and you can recreate those pages for yourself so you'll have as many blank pages to write on as you like. You could get a journal or notebook and use that.

Whatever works for you is the right way to do it!

At the end of each chapter, you'll find a section called Manifesting Moments.

In an effort to push you past 'pretty confident' and into 'sign me up,' I thought it might be interesting to talk to all sorts of people in my life and find out their thoughts on manifesting and how they made it work for them.

I asked each of them what the word "manifesting" evokes for them and how the process operates in their lives. Their answers are smart and inspiring and even funny. And all of them helped me to think about the many ways manifesting can work through and be integrated into our lives.

If their stories speak to you, you might consider jotting down favorite sections or highlighting them to revisit. Nothing better than a real-life manifesting moment to help inform your own journey.

Here's an example of a manifesting moment to whet your appetite for what's to come:

My friend Celeste doesn't believe in manifesting, but she does believe in the power of a positive attitude, particularly with a faith component. I say it's all the same: miracle, magic, prayer, energy, gratitude attitude. Many roads, one destination.

There are so many unseen facets of life on planet Earth; I often grapple with these unknowns and unknowables. If manifesting really works, I have trouble understanding why so many humans are suffering from malnutrition, hunger, poverty, depression, disease, displacement, and discrimination. It seems like we, the privileged few, are able to sit in our comfortable homes with full bellies, thinking about manifestation while the rest of the planet suffers. Like, shouldn't they be able to manifest clean water and safe neighborhoods for themselves? That sounds dangerously like expecting them to pull themselves up by their own bootstraps. I don't like it and I don't get it.

But what I do know is that we can let the universe know what we need and want, and the universe listens. (Tribute to a Melissa Etheridge song!)

My mother told me years ago to be careful what you ask for, and never to ask for money. She prayed for money during a particularly difficult time (as a single mother teaching in an underfunded urban school while raising four teenagers) and received what she needed when her only and beloved aunt, Aunt Teds, died. This warning kept me away from what I now called manifesting for several years.

I now see it differently. Teds was close to eighty; she was seemingly in good health, but our bodies give out eventually. Teds was a single gal who lived on Long Island and worked in the city as an executive secretary. She was frugal and classy and saved her money carefully. I'm sure Teds planned to pass her life savings on to her nieces when the time came—

which it did in 1981. My mother was filled with grief and good old Catholic guilt, but in the big picture, Teds got to die peacefully in her sleep (and isn't that what most of us hope for?) and my mom got the financial boost she needed. It makes sense to me.

When it comes to manifesting, what works for me is to get really clear about the parameters: clear my mind, visualize the goal or desire, express gratitude for all the good things, set any limits ("Hey out there! I need ten grand, but I don't want anyone to die in the process!"), and let it go out into the universe, just like that. That's how I picture it. Open my hands and my heart, and let it go with a sprinkling of stardust and a boost of joy. Repeating it is a good idea, whenever the idea strikes, sometimes over days or months.

It may sound easy, but it's a real challenge to keep it pure and non-greedy and filled with gratitude. Meditating before, during and after helps me, too. (Although meditation is super hard for me since I'm often easily distracted—ooh, squirrel!—but that's another topic.)

Maybe this is my brain's way of keeping me on track and nudging me to make decisions which eventually get me to the goal. And that's okay! I have no control over the process. Once I set it free, I trust the universe (God, Goddess, Allah, Yahweh, the

Great Unknown, the Great Spaghetti Monster, Woo) to arrange the particulars. It can be scary, trusting that good things are coming but not knowing where, when, or how—very scary. I have to be careful not to dwell in that fear, because that's a showstopper for sure. The universe has a way of bringing those challenges involving dread and fear right to the fore. "Oh, you never wanted to be an Early Childhood Center Director? Well, here's your chance! Face those fears!" Ugh! "You're terrified that your daughter's mental health challenges will only get worse and even more unmanageable? Here ya go!"

I believe we receive these negative "gifts" because the universe knows our emotions, but perhaps cannot interpret the difference between joyful, pure desires and the dark terrors in our hearts. Maybe emotions are all the same outside of the physical realm. I just don't know.

—**Kaye H.**, Fern Festie (a.k.a. my festie bestie)

CHAPTER ONE

~~~~~~~~~~

YOU HOLD THE SECRET TO MANIFESTING YOUR DESIRES

If You Are Willing to Ask for Anything, You Just Might Find Yourself Getting Everything

I am so happy you have decided to start this journey. No matter where it takes you, I know it will be a welcome adventure. If you're feeling nervous or unsure, don't worry. Although some of the steps might feel awkward the first time around, they'll be second nature in no time. The best part is this: you already hold the secret to it all.

And since this is the first round, here's a little how-to reminder:

Say the mantra in your head. Then repeat the mantra out loud. Ask yourself the question and answer it in your head. Do that until you work through the entire list of questions. End by reciting the mantra once more in your head and then once more out loud. Then, write it down somewhere. You can keep a little notepad or journal nearby or even use the notes app on your phone. At some later point, share the mantra; maybe tell your partner, your friend, or your mom. That last step can really energize you to make it real.

I am a badass.

I hold the secret to being a badass.

What makes me feel badass today?

I am a badass.

I hold the secret to being a badass.

What fear will I face today?

I am a badass.

I hold the secret to being a badass.

What can I do today to make me feel even more badass?

I am a badass.

I hold the secret to being a badass.

What fellow badass can I connect with today?

> I am a badass.
>
> I hold the secret to being a badass.
>
> Why is being a badass important to me?
>
> I am a badass.
>
> I hold the secret to being a badass.

The secret is simple: the secret is you. In some ways, this feels like the biggest hurdle to overcome when it comes to accepting and projecting the badass you are. If everyone can be a badass, why don't they? If I'm such a badass, why don't I have it all? If someone like me can be a badass, is being a badass really a thing?

It's the biggest hurdle and the biggest secret of all. There is no hurdle and there is no secret. Any hurdle is the one you are creating, and any secret is that most can't/won't/don't accept that we can do the thing. We just have to, well, *do* "the thing."

I was lucky. My dad taught me early on that I absolutely can do "the thing."

I'm not sure how old I was at the time—in my mind, maybe nine or ten. I was at the Orioles game at the old Memorial Stadium in Baltimore, Maryland. It was just me and my dad, just like every year. It was my birthday. We would go see a game and then get a bushel of crabs to crack and eat in the backyard.

The seats weren't any good. But I didn't care. At the time, I probably didn't even realize they weren't good seats. All I cared about was being together, just me and my dad, on my birthday.

That year, as we sat in the stands, my dad turned to me and smiled. He asked if I was ready. "Ready for what?" I asked. "A little challenge," he said. He handed me the empty Coleman drink cooler we had brought along, presumably to fill with water at my mother's instruction. "Take this to one of the vendors and ask them to fill it with ice," he said. "Okay!" I said.

"And..." he added, "if you can get them to fill it with Coke too, I'll get you the ice cream sundae that comes in the little mini baseball helmet," he said.

I can only imagine how wide my eyes looked at the thought. I can still imagine the fear, excitement, delight, and thrill. Going on an errand alone? Asking someone to give me something for no reason? The prized baseball ice cream sundae that my mom had always said no to at previous games?

I could not believe my luck. But I also could not imagine managing what at that moment seemed like a Herculean task. So I took a deep breath, grabbed that red Coleman cooler, and headed over to the concessions.

I walked around for a few minutes checking out the different stands. Most of them sold the same things or variations of the same: peanuts, hot dogs, lemonade, ice cream, soda, nachos. Finally, I said to my grade-school-aged self, "You have to just go for it. Daddy wouldn't have sent you if he didn't think you could do it."

"Excuse me," I said to the man behind the counter. "May I have some ice?" I held up the red cooler. The man smiled at me and said, "Of course you can." His friendly demeanor made me feel instantly more confident. I thanked him and inquired if he was having a good day. The man seemed surprised by the inquiry. "People rarely ask me that," he said. "I ask them. But..." I smiled and asked, "So, are you?"

He laughed. "I am! How about you?" I told him I was having a great day. "My dad let me come get ice by myself and..." Suddenly I wasn't sure I could do it. "And what?" he asked.

"Well, he said if I could get Coke in that cooler too, he'd buy me one of those sundaes in the helmets!" I got overexcited and said it a little too loudly, I'm sure. The man laughed, and I am sure my face did nothing to mask my embarrassment. "Well, I would never stand in the way of a girl and her sundae!" he told me and started to fill the cooler with Coke, having just added the ice.

"And it's my birthday!" I blurted out. "Well why didn't you say that in the first place?" the man said, now laughing and smiling at what must have been the funniest exchange of his day. "There you go!" he said, handing me the cooler. "Happy birthday! And tell your dad he's very lucky to have a daughter like you." I thanked him and waved as I started racing back to my dad.

"I did it!" I yelled when I got back to our seats. I remember the other people in the stands laughing. I wonder now if they thought I had just gone to pee or something.

"Coke?" my dad asked. "Yup!" I said. "Excellent job, kiddo," my dad said. "Do you know why he did that for you?"

I told him I had no idea. "Because you asked," he told me. "But what if everyone asked?" I wondered, screwing up my face in disbelief. "But they don't. Not for that, not in that way," he explained. "Most importantly, though, not everyone is you." I started to question him. "But..." I started to say. "Did you tell the truth?" my dad asked. I nodded. "Did you ask how his day was?" I nodded. "Did you make him smile and laugh?" More nodding. "Were you kind?" More nodding.

"Were you pretending?" my dad asked me. "Pretending?" I asked. "To be kind," my father replied. "Of course not," I told him. "That's why, Jenny," my father said. "The universe rewards us for being good people. It rewards us for being ourselves. Too many people don't treat other people the way they should. That is the secret—to everything. Got it?" "Got it," I confirmed. "So...ice cream?" "Yes," my dad laughed. "Ice cream."

I'm sure I didn't fully understand the breadth and depth of that lesson at the time. But I can tell you one thing for sure: He was right. He was teaching me the way of the badass. He didn't call it that, of course. But a badass walks through life with kindness and confidence.

I manifested that cooler full of ice and Coke—and that ice cream sundae, for that matter—by trusting myself and trusting that the universe would reward my true intentions. It's not about tricking anyone or lying; it's old school. "Ask and it will be given to you; seek and you will find; knock and the door will be opened to you."

I don't get everything and anything I want. I
don't get everything I ask for. And I don't ask for
everything I want. That last part is on me. But the
rest is about how the universe works. Not everything
is meant for everyone. It's like that country song,
"Thank God for Unanswered Prayers," or that old
saying, "Be careful what you wish for—you just
might get it."

Sometimes, we are literally asking for things,
like a cooler full of Coke and ice. But other times,
we are more vague, too vague, when it comes to
asking for what we want. We ask for happiness, for
comfort, for security. But how is the universe to
know just what we are asking for? Rain makes some
people happy. Being in bed makes some people
comfortable. Staying on at the same job nearly
forever makes some people feel secure. But are
those the outcomes *you* are seeking? We may not
even know we're not being clear or intentional while
we're doing this. But this kind of mistake might
just be what is keeping us from manifesting our
badass selves.

If you never apply for that job, you are asking not
to get it.

If you never ask someone out, you are asking them
not to date you.

If you never save a nickel, you are asking to have an empty account.

If you never engage with the world around you, you are asking for emptiness.

If it sounds harsh, I'm sorry. The truth is not covered in glitter and sequins. Sometimes it's hard to hear. But often, that's also why it's important to hear.

Take a minute. Take a breath. Ask yourself:

What am I asking for via my actions and thoughts?

Now listen to the answer. Really listen.

I keep saying I want to publish a novel. That's what I really want. But I haven't worked on it in a year. So if it's really what I want, then that's some lousy manifesting on my part. I am not going to have a novel published if I am not even showing the universe my good intentions by writing it.

"Ask and ye shall receive," right? But of course, that doesn't mean simply saying, "Can I have my novel published please?" We ask the universe by showing it that we are intended for the thing for which we are asking.

If I wrote every day, if I focused my energies, if I was honest with myself and the universe, and the desire was pure and clear, I bet I could—*would*—publish a novel one day.

It's not just "I think I can." It's "I think I can and I am." It's different.

A lot of manifesting falls short because it looks like my dad on that first day of his religious studies class. "If manifesting is real, make a million dollars drop from the sky." Nope. Rule one: The laws of physics still—at least in most cases—exist. You have to work within the system. But you also have to work.

Now, in contrast to the novel example, when I really wanted to headline a comedy show, I took every gig—unpaid as well as paid—and I showed up. And I put myself in a position where people who could make that headliner gig happen could see me. I put it out in the ether. I kept saying it to anyone and everyone who would listen, "What I really want is to headline a comedy show."

Then, two summers ago, when I was emceeing a music festival, someone who owned a bar said, "You're great up there. Want to do a show at my club?"

I manifested that. I made that happen. I lined up my ducks, and I asked.

You have to be ready and you have to be willing to ask all the questions.

You have to ask yourself, "What do I really want, and how am I showing that to be true?"

You have to ask the permission givers—the vendor, the club owner, the potential date.

You have to ask the universe, "Is this what you have in store for me?"

If you are willing to ask for anything, you just might find yourself getting everything.

That's badass manifesting. Say it with me now.

I hold the secret to being a badass.

I am a badass.

You sure are!

Manifesting Moments

"To me, the word 'manifesting' means holding something in one's secret thoughts so steadily that it creates an energy that is almost magnetic, and that energy brings that thing or that reality into one's life. It's believing something very fully.

The thing I think of first when I think of having manifested in my own life was getting a pet monkey, because I was reading about them and picturing myself holding one and being really good friends with one for probably a year and a half. And then I got one.

It was something that I remember thinking about so vividly for so long; but then when it came into my life, I cried.

I would imagine that I'm also manifesting all the time and don't even know it. And then there was the number one, a manifestation session with you, Jenny Block, winning the raffle, the big award money, so you could give it right back to The Land. So cool.

And Judy. I started praying for the perfect dog for me and tried to feel the feelings that I would feel when I knew that I had the perfect dog for me, and then two weeks later—bam—there she was."

—Mollie Rose, singer/songwriter

"Manifesting to me is creating an image of something so strongly that it becomes my reality. Manifesting is my way of life. Since life can throw so many curveballs, I see manifestation as taking that curveball and hitting it out of the park."

—Kristan Serafino, celebrity hairdresser and inventor and founder of The Best Paste

"Manifesting is setting an intention in the world. It could be through prayer, meditation, or journaling. We can manifest through our desire that the universe hears our thoughts. I believe that manifesting is setting that intention.

I would say that I have manifested, but I would like to think that I've done it in a different way. I don't know if you've ever heard of the Human Design system, but when I took that test, it talked about how I manifest with this openhanded mindset. I'm not necessarily specific on what I want, but I open myself to whatever the universe is meant to send my way.

And I would say that my whole life is an aspect
of that manifestation. I mean, I look at my
photography career and how I set out to do hotel
photography. I manifested that living in New York
and happened to get a job working as a hotel social
media representative for the last year and a half.
There are, I believe, so many more examples of
manifestation being prevalent in my life, but in the
end, I believe if my energy is continuously being put
toward good, that is its own form of manifestation."

—Alexandrea Foster, photographer

CHAPTER TWO

~~~~~~~~~

THE ONLY PERMISSION YOU NEED TO MANIFEST YOUR DREAMS COMES FROM YOU

If You Are the One to Give Yourself Permission, You Will Always Have Permission

This is your journey. You don't need anyone else to tell you whether or not it's a worthy one or how you should start it. So much in life requires permission, so much has rules and constraints. Not here. This is your manifesting experience, and I am here to simply guide and support. You don't need my permission or anyone else's to make it happen. So say yes to yourself and make it happen.

I am a badass.

I don't need anyone else's permission to
be a badass.

What makes me feel badass today?

I am a badass.

I don't need anyone else's permission to
be a badass.

What fear will I face today?

I am a badass.

I don't need anyone else's permission to
be a badass.

What can I do today to make me feel even
more badass?

I am a badass.

I don't need anyone else's permission to
be a badass.

What fellow badass can I connect with today?

I am a badass.

I don't need anyone else's permission to
be a badass.

Why is being a badass important to me?

I am a badass.

I don't need anyone else's permission to
be a badass.

There is no one else in this equation but me. I am always judge and jury. Looking inward is always the right answer.

This issue of approval has always been a little hard for me. I feel like my whole life I've picked jobs and hobbies alike that require permission: being in a play, writing for publication, attending a writing workshop. For others, it might be things like playing a team sport, appearing on television, or participating in a certain program. You get the idea.

And sure, there are always ways around that. Start your own team. Pick a school with a high admission rate. Start your own YouTube channel. Self-publish. I get all of that. But if you're anything like me, the permission thing is part and parcel of achieving your goals. It's only feels worth it if not everyone can join, play, be a participant, or whatever.

But this is not true when it comes to being a badass. There is no training or sign-up. There's no test or audition. There's no limited number of seats. You get to step into being a badass if you so choose.

This might seem like a little thing; but it was huge to me to realize this. And even though I know it to be true, sometimes I need a reminder, which I got recently at a Taylor Swift concert, of all places.

My incredibly sweet friend Clark managed to snap up six tickets to the show in Houston and invited me and my wife and daughter along for the adventure.

We all meticulously planned our outfits months in advance; I started beading the now famous, colorful bracelets like my life depended on it. My house was covered in beads. For the uninitiated, in her song, "You're on Your Own, Kid," Taylor Swift sings, "So, make the friendship bracelets, take the moment and taste it. You've got no reason to be afraid."

Suddenly, Swifties everywhere were making bracelets and trading them at shows. Adorably, some raver went public claiming credit, saying ravers started the phenom in the 90s exchanging "kandi," as they called the bracelets they traded with each other. But those of us raised in the 70s know that summer camp kids and Girl Scouts started that tradition before anyone ever dreamed up furry leg warmers and unicorn headbands for grown-ups.

On the big night of the show, my daughter and I donned matching dresses and our custom jean jackets with Taylor's lyrics from "This Is Why We Can't Have Nice Things" emblazoned on the back. "And here's to my mama," my daughter's read; "Had to listen to all this drama," mine said. I pulled on my unicorn boots just like the ones Taylor wore in her video for "Calm Down," and I filled both my arms with bracelets from wrist to elbow.

I was so excited until we started walking toward the stadium. Suddenly, I was filled with the same dread I felt when I was thirteen years old, headed to my cabin at camp, excitedly wearing my new Care Bears T-shirt, before learning that "Care Bears is for little kids," as the mean girls quickly informed me before laughing and running off in their Bon Jovi T-shirts and Jordache jeans.

All I could think at that moment was, "Who gave you permission to wear this outfit and make these silly bracelets? Who do you think you are? You don't think you're one of the cool girls, do you?" I could actually hear myself cruelly laughing at myself in my own head.

So, I shook my head and got myself together, and I reminded myself that the boss of me is—me. I gave myself permission to twin with my twentysomething daughter. I gave myself permission to giddily exchange bracelets with anyone I choose. I gave myself permission to scream and cry and sing every lyric at the top of my lungs. And once permission was granted, I was off to the races. I had the best time, and I enjoyed watching everyone around me having the best time too.

No one had been or was judging me but me, and no one had been or was withholding permission but me.

Remember, withholding permission is the ultimate means of control. As long as you think you need someone else's approval to live and be and express yourself, you are allowing outside forces to control you. But as the saying goes, the only things we all have to abide are death and taxes. The rest is in your control.

That's much easier at a Taylor Swift concert, where everyone is there with one focus. Everyone present shares at least one thing—a love for someone who is an incredibly talented writer and musician as well as a truly kind and sparkly human. It's a place steeped in love and support. The real world, of course, is not so much like that most of the time.

But that's all the more reason to stay grounded in the fact that you don't need anyone's permission but your own to manifest a badass life. And you have the right and the responsibility to grant yourself that permission.

You can apply for that job. You can choose that paint color. You can wear that outfit. You can listen to and love that music. You can take up that hobby. You can go to that movie. You can see that play. You can join that conversation. You can dance at that wedding. You can explore that museum. You can travel to that place. You can take that adventure.

It makes me so sad—and mad—when I see those "What not to wear over forty" articles, or comments like, "I can't believe she would go there/do that/wear those." What I hear between the lines when I read those comments is, "I am so insecure about my desires. I have to manage the desires of others because of how they do/wear/enjoy/listen to/go to those things, which means I could as well, and I'm too scared—therefore it's better to put them down and make them feel bad so I don't have to feel bad."

It's shitty. I don't like it. And I don't tolerate it.

"The worst kind of person is someone who makes you feel bad, dumb, or stupid for being excited about something."
—Taylor Swift

I am the boss of me.

I get to decide.

I give the permission.

It's something I worked very hard on with my own daughter, who is now in her twenties. I remember when she was little and I asked her to get dressed so

we could go the store. She asked if she could wear a
tutu with her Ugg boots and a rainbow sweatshirt.
"Will you be comfortable?" I asked her. "Yes," she
told me with the sweetest grin on her face.

Then I asked her this: "Do you care if other people
look at you and make a funny face?" In reply, she
asked me why anyone would do that. "Because
most people are boring and dress how they think
other people want them to dress, but you're letting
your heart choose. Some people don't get that," I
explained to her.

"That's sad, mommy," she said. "I'm going to go put
on my tutu." And with that, she raced up the stairs,
and all day, whenever she caught anyone's eye,
she gave them a giant smile, waved to them, and
declared, "My heart picked my outfit!"

I wonder sometimes if that stuck with some people.
I hope so. It sure stuck with me. She's still like that
now. She wears what she wants, eats what she
wants, and watches what she wants. She's polite,
smart, kind, and respectful. But she doesn't seek
out or wait for anyone's permission to be who she is,
even though she knows there are people who wish
she would.

It's my wish for everyone to feel that empowered.
But it can be hard depending on how you were raised

or what your life experiences have been. Traditional schooling certainly doesn't help; you can't even use the bathroom without asking. And all too many workplaces are like that too, micromanaging people into feeling like they have no authority and no autonomy.

Sadly, that can seep into one's personal life as well. Too many women think they need a man's permission. Too many adult children still think they need their parents' permission. Permission or approval, whatever you want to call it, you don't need it. As long as no one—including you—is being hurt, you get to decide what kind of badass person you want to be and the badass life you want to manifest.

What would you do? Where would you go? What would you explore? What would you try? What would you wear? Eat? Listen to or watch? You know that old saying, "Dance like no one's watching"? You're allowed to *live* like no one's watching, because even if they are, and even if they are judging you or otherwise withholding permission for you to show up and exist as your authentic self, it's only because they feel trapped by the inauthentic life they have, for which they have no one to blame but themselves.

That's their stuff. That's not your stuff. Your stuff is
to manifest your badass self in a way that feels like
you and to manifest what the universe has in store
for you. Being inauthentic is as dangerous as—or
maybe even more dangerous than—being negative.
Both will block your true path.

You are the boss of you. And if that's not literally
true, you need to make some changes, because
no one else should be controlling or mandating or
dictating your choices—period.

You are a badass.

You don't need anyone else's permission to
be a badass.

Say it out loud now—

I am a badass.

I don't need anyone else's permission to be a badass.

You sure don't!

Manifesting Moments

"Manifesting to me means connecting with the universe and being open to changes. To me, manifesting is our true inner thoughts being reflected in our daily realities. So, whatever those true inner thoughts are will manifest in the way we live. I feel like my entire life has been manifested, good and bad. If I am intentional about my thoughts and want a specific result in my life, then it takes discipline and patience to maintain the same inner thoughts and narrative to manifest the results I want."

—Emily LaRosa, attorney

"For me, manifesting is repetitively setting an intention or goal, out loud, written, or in your mind. The act of aligning your conscious and subconscious mind will help guide you in making choices, actions, and decisions that lead you toward that goal. I don't believe in divine intervention there, but this simple act helps unconsciously guide you."

—Johnny Ray Noon, Commercial Real Estate Executive

"I've manifested many things in my life, and what does it mean to me? It means that when we put our subconscious in a state where we envision what we want to come into our life, with concentration and positive thoughts, we have the ability to manifest it. We can make it happen! We can make it *real*!"

—Linda Janowski, entrepreneur

"Manifesting to me means making something happen, either positively or negatively. It means giving energy to a possible outcome! I manifest all the time by actively thinking and visualizing said outcome. I do this passively while driving, showering, or walking my dog. But when I'm really intentional about it, I write it down, create a vision board, pray about it, and even speak it aloud to friends or out in the open. Bottom line, when I really want something, I get it expressed so it is outside of my head as much as it is in my head."

—Becca Jones, creative techie

"The word 'manifest' means magic and the power of positive thought! There have been a lot of collaborations in business that maybe I manifested, maybe I followed up on email a lot of times, maybe I was consistent in what I was trying to do, but if all of that is manifesting, then I'll keep doing it. I will say, when I met Anthony, my husband, friends of mine were like, 'Of course this is your guy—he's exactly your type! You manifested him!' "

—Julie Mollo, founder and designer at Julie Mollo

"Manifesting to me is 'birthing into reality.' As a young girl, I used to look in the mirror and do 'pretend' live shots for the news, even though I didn't think I was really pretty enough. Years later, after I entered the business, I realized, 'It's not about how you look, but what you do!' Technically, I had been doing it for a while. What was happening in the mirror manifested itself on the television screen."

—Deborah Duncan, host and senior producer of *Great Day Houston* at CBS affiliate KHOU-11

CHAPTER THREE

~~~~~~~~

IT'S OKAY TO QUESTION YOUR JOURNEY BECAUSE YOU KNOW THE ANSWERS

If I Can Ask the Question, I Can Find the Answer

This isn't easy or simple, I get that. It might even be a little scary. That's okay too. You might start asking yourself, "Why am I doing this?" "Can this really work?" "Am I capable of this?" "What if this is stupid?" When that happens, take a deep breath, think about what you want most in the world, and remind yourself that you've got this. Questioning is fine. Just know the answer is always within you—*always*.

I am a badass.

It's okay that sometimes I question my badassery.

What makes me feel badass today?

I am a badass.

It's okay that sometimes I question my badassery.

What fear will I face today?

I am a badass.

It's okay that sometimes I question my badassery.

What can I do today to make me feel even more badass?

I am a badass.

It's okay that sometimes I question my badassery.

What fellow badass can I connect with today?

I am a badass.

It's okay that sometimes I question my badassery.

Why is being a badass important to me?

I am a badass.

It's okay that sometimes I question my badassery.

I promise it really is okay.

When you ask yourself if you are a badass, the answer is always yes.

But badasses question their own badassery too. It's a fact of life. And it's not necessarily a bad thing. It can keep you on the path you want to be on and help you stay out of the weeds.

Even if I don't feel like a badass today, today is just one day. A feeling is not a reality.

There have been many times in my life when I did not feel like a badass, times when I questioned my own badassery. When I was a kid, however, I thought I was the queen of the world.

I thought of myself as popular in my elementary and middle school years. I saw myself as well-liked. I had lots of friends. I had a boyfriend when I was thirteen. I got asked to school dances. I had always been funny and smart and nice, traits that my parents had assured me were the ones in which people were interested. But the summer before high school was a whole other story, one that proved to be an accurate foreshadowing of what the next four years would bring.

I'd been going to Camp Louise every summer for as long as I can remember. It was an all-girls camp in the Catoctin Mountains, sitting right on the state line between Cascade, Maryland, and Waynesboro, Pennsylvania. It was an arts camp really; it had a theatre-in-the-round outdoor solarium and the best arts and crafts department a kid could want. I loved it there.

That is, except for the summer of 1983—the summer I turned thirteen. I arrived at camp as I always did with my huge, black camp trunk with the silver hinges and lock. It was filled with shorts and T-shirts, bug spray, and card games. But it didn't take me long to realize that the other girls were whispering to one another and giggling behind their hands as they watched me unpack.

I was still completely unaware of what was so funny, so I continued hanging up my Smurf memo board and Strawberry Shortcake calendar. I unpacked my white crew socks and my no-name white canvas tennis shoes. It was weird. No one really said hi to me. But I just figured they were all busy. I guessed. Then the counselors came into the bunk.

"Okay, girls, everyone on their bunk," Holly said. "Welcome back to another great summer at Camp Louise." Everyone clapped and cheered. "As you know, living with the same fourteen girls in a cabin for eight weeks isn't always easy. So let's be respectful of each other and each other's spaces, okay?" Everyone nodded.

"Now," said Sarah, the other counselor, "let's go around and introduce ourselves. Tell us your name, where you're from, and what you hope to do this summer." We went around in a circle. "I'm Alexis. I'm from Randallstown," one girl said. "Randallstown rocks!" someone yelled, and several girls clapped and cheered.

"Okay, girls, let's settle down. Let Alexis talk," Holly, said. "I hope to be in the plays," Alexis said. "That's a big shocker," one girl teased. Alexis smiled; she was always the lead. Every summer the camp put on two major productions and Alexis was always the lead: Dorothy, Miriam the Librarian, Daisy Mae, Sandy. You get the picture.

"Okay," said Sarah. "That's great! Who's next?" "I'm Heather. I'm from Randallstown. And this summer I hope to marry Jon Bon Jovi." All of the girls started rolling on their bunks with laughter. Even the counselors were laughing. I wasn't laughing. I didn't know who Jon Bon Jovi was.

"I'm Rachel. I'm from Catonsville. And I hope to spend as much time at Airy this summer as possible." Airy was the boys' camp. All of the girls smiled at one another, nodding in agreement. Airy? I was thinking. We hate going to Airy. The boys tease us. The counselors make us dance with the boys there. It was so stupid. Eventually it was my turn.

"My name is Jenny, and this is Hairy. Hairy and I are from Bel Air, and we hope to be in the plays too," I said. Around my neck and waist were the arms and legs of a skinny stuffed monkey—Hairy. The girls made faces at one another, shaking their heads and rolling their eyes. If I could have swallowed Hairy whole to make him disappear, I would have.

"That's great!" Sarah tried to save the swiftly sinking situation. "Okay, rules." She went on to tick off all of the rules, but I didn't hear a word she said. My brain was on overdrive. What had happened? What had I done wrong? I'd been going to camp with most of these girls for years. We always brought our stuffed animals.

I had been sure they'd think Hairy and I were hilarious. I slumped down, trying to make myself as invisible as possible for the rest of the meeting. As the counselors talked, I looked around the room. It was like being on another planet. Instead of Muppets stickers and Care Bear posters, there were signed rock concert tickets of bands I had never heard of, and posters of guys, actors and singers I couldn't identify if my life depended on it.

I didn't really know what to make of it. I just knew
I was in foreign terrain. And so it went for the rest
of the summer. It was a cruel introduction into
what I would soon discover was the "real world" of
teenagers: Bonnie Belle Lipsmackers and lavender
Maybelline eye shadow; curling irons and hair dryers
with diffusers; designer clothes and rhinestone
encrusted sneakers; and gossiping, cliques,
and dieting.

It was territory I was in no way prepared to navigate.
I didn't read Teen Beat, and my mother didn't think
that my underwear needed to have "Bloomies"
printed across the backside. I didn't even know
they *made* underwear with "Bloomies" printed
across the back.

I managed to salvage the summer. I was in the plays.
And I made friends with other girls who appeared to
be as clueless as I seemed to be.

But the whole experience left me a little raw. I
started questioning myself for all of the wrong
reasons. To be honest, it kicked me off course for
a bit. I found myself trying to follow those bands,
wear what other girls wore, and listen to the music
the cool kids preferred. But it just didn't work for
me. It felt inauthentic because, well, it was.

The weirdest part is that when you question your badassery and try to act like someone else who *seems* like a badass, you actually come across as less badass. This is because it's next to impossible to feel and act strong and confident when you're playing a role.

So, instead of feeling inadequate when you question whether or not you really are a badass, think instead about who you are "trying" to align yourself with or what you're "trying" to be. "Do or do not. There is no try." Yes, I am quoting a tiny green guy from a sci-fi film. But he's not wrong. If you are trying, you're not doing.

It's okay to question yourself. It's not okay to allow that questioning to set you on a path that's not meant for you.

Impostor syndrome is a real thing, and it can sneak up on you any time. I applied to the MFA program at NYU—twice. And I was rejected—twice. That definitely made me question myself. "You're a badass, huh? Really? You can't even get into grad school."

The truth is I wasn't able to get into *that* grad school at *that* time with *that* writing sample. It took me a couple of days to process having been turned down. But it was vital that I come to terms with what had really happened rather than what my brain was trying to trick me into thinking had happened.

What had happened was that I had not been admitted into NYU at that time.

What my brain was trying to convince me of was that I wasn't good enough and would never be good enough, and what's even the point if I'm not good enough?

That's a lot.

But setbacks, big or small, can feel insurmountable. It can feel like that one thing cancels out everything else. But still...

I am a badass.

It's okay that sometimes I question my badassery.

When I question myself, I also challenge myself to unpack what I am feeling.

Was this meant for me?

Was this the time for me?

Is this aligned with who I actually am?

Is the closing of this path intended to put me on another?

Being a badass is perhaps more than anything about being self-aware enough to know that nothing just falls in your lap and that not everything is meant for you even though you might think it is. If it is meant to be, it will be.

When I don't get the story, when I don't get invited, when I don't get accepted, I question myself first. But when I'm done with that, I question the path. If not this, then what? And I do my very best to use that questioning to find my way.

Do I try again?

Do I do it differently?

Do I close this chapter?

Do I seek help?

You are a badass. You have to trust that for starters. That means that one of the most important tools in your toolbox is using setbacks and disappointments to refuel you and get you to where you want to be—where you are meant to be.

I interviewed Broadway star, Chayanne Jackson, who grew up with nothing; no running water, an outhouse instead of a bathroom. He had no access. He had no role models. But he could sing, and he knew he could sing. And he trusted that singing was what he was put on Earth to do. So now that's what he does.

"How did you think this life was possible considering how and where you grew up?" I asked him. "I guess I manifested it," he replied. I almost fell off the sofa. I was in the middle of writing this book when that conversation happened. It was like the little bird I needed in my ear.

No one expects you to be 100 percent confident or sure of yourself all of the time. But the through line in that star's life was knowing who he was, what he wanted, and where he belonged. *Everything* he did was in pursuit of that goal. Imagine if you put 100 percent of your energy toward the one thing you really wanted…

That includes when you question yourself. Take that questioning and put it to work.

Why didn't I get it?

Was it really what I wanted?

If it was, what can I do differently next time?

The difference between someone who is a badass and someone who isn't is that a badass knows everything is okay: the questions, the missteps, the failures—all of it. Everything is a step toward our goal if we use it for that. The only person who can allow the questioning to consume you is you.

The haters we encounter along the way love for us to question ourselves because that's what they do. A hater is constantly questioning their own worth and then lashing out at others. When you agree to make yourself small, they can feel bigger.

Don't make yourself smaller.

Say it with me—

I am a badass.

It's okay that sometimes I question my badassery.

It sure is!

Manifesting Moments

"I love the idea of speaking the positive reality as if it was in my life now. The names of each of the folders on my phone are all manifestations. So all of my money apps are in the 'I am rich' folder, and all of my mobile and travel apps—my maps, my Uber, my Lyft, anything to do with being able to move around—are in a folder called 'I am able,' recognizing for example 'being able' to walk. Any of them that are about dating, including dating apps or hookup apps, go under 'I am loved.' All of my communication apps are in the one called 'I am articulate.'

So I'm looking at manifesting every single day. I really love calling in the reality of 'I have abundance.' And what the *Sex Magic* podcast has taught me is go to the place where you feel it; and then beyond just feeling it, what does it feel like to wake up that day as someone wealthy? What do you imagine your life would be like? If I had the wealth that I wanted, what would that mean? Once you have envisioned that, the next step is to explore it and lean into it. And then I start to get little visions of what it looks like."

—Timothy Westbrook, designer, TL Brooke

"Did you ever see *Halloweentown*? 'Magic is really very simple, all you've got to do is want something and then let yourself have it,' as Aggie Cromwell states in *Halloweentown*. Manifesting works the same way: Want something and let yourself have it. When practicing gratitude, try being thankful for something you have not yet received."

—Darla Belflower, CEO of Belflower Training and Consultation

"Manifesting to me is creating a map to where you want to be or what you want in life. Evoking or recalling all of my past experiences and knowledge helps me stay on the path. I have manifested every experience in my adult life, but I have learned to not have the expectation of getting exactly what I want. Sometimes shit goes south, but it's in essence what I asked for."

—Charlette Henager, creative director of Her Own Life

CHAPTER FOUR

~~~~~~~~~

YOU KNOW YOUR BADASS SELF AND YOU HAVE NO REASON TO HIDE IT

If You Know Who You Are, No One Can Take That Away from You

You know. You know who you are and what you really want. Sometimes you might feel far away from both of those things; but deep down, you know. And no matter what other people say or do, no matter where life does—or does not—take you, you are still that person and you still have those dreams. You deserve to live in that truth. You deserve to be your whole, authentic self and to live a full, authentic life. Trust that. Trust yourself. And trust this process.

I am a badass.

I know myself.

What makes me feel badass today?

I am a badass.

I know myself.

What fear will I face today?

I am a badass.

I know myself.

What can I do today to make me feel even more badass?

I am a badass.

I know myself.

What fellow badass can I connect with today?

I am a badass.

I know myself.

Why is being a badass important to me?

I am a badass.

I know myself.

You know who you are. You may question it at times, but you know. And who you are is not defined by something external. You are not your job, your house, your belongings, your family, or your friends. You are who you are, independent of all of that.

Being a badass is who I am, not what I do. Being a badass is not dependent on anything. No matter what happens, no one can take your badassery away from you.

The problem with letting external things define you and your badassery is that they can always disappear or be taken away.

You can't always control whether or not you're working and what you're doing for or at work. I have had *so* many jobs. Some have been much more badass than others, at least on paper. But I am still a badass despite slinging buckets of beer or changing diapers. In fact, I think being able to stay secure in your badass identity despite your work makes you even *more* of a badass—not less of one. Being a badass movie star is easy compared to being a badass hotel maid. The latter is tougher but it is far from impossible.

It's not the work you do that makes you a badass. It's how you do that work—whatever it is—and how you regroup when the situation demands it.

When COVID came along, a lot of my writing work dried up. There were no shows or concerts to review; no celebrities to interview about events or performances people should go see; no restaurants to try out and write about their food. There were no places to travel to; so there was nowhere to write about. And I felt guilty about being upset that my work was drying up when people all over the world were sick and dying.

My fourth book was released right as the world was shutting down, and so my book tour—and consequently sales—were shut down too. And again, I felt guilty being mad about my book not getting its grand entrance into the world when we were all facing a pandemic with no end in sight. I wanted to curl into a ball and just call it a day. And I did, for a minute.

Then I started looking outside the frame. It's like looking at a photo or a painting, and instead of focusing on the image in front of you, you imagine what's going on just outside the edges of that frame. As I started to look around, I saw that the earth was still turning; for example, people were still getting married.

I saw one couple talking on Facebook about getting married at a drive-in movie theater, and I thought, "That's an interesting and uplifting story!" So, with the help of an online writer's group, I got the email address of an editor at the *New York Times*, and within three days, I had my very first assignment. That was in April of 2020.

I have been writing for them ever since. And it is a dream. I get to dwell on love stories and share them with the world. I manifested the perfect gig for myself.

Here's the thing, I may have to remind myself of it sometimes, but I am a girl who gets things done. That's a complete sentence. The how or when or even why is not really important. It's about getting the damn thing done. And that's what I do.

I do my best to remember that, and I hope you will too. Because as soon as the next thing comes up, it can be easy to forget how you did all of those other things. But don't forget: Your past is your badass superpower. Because despite it all, you make things happen.

Sometimes you might not get all of the things done, or maybe you do, but it's not the stuff you had on your list for that day. The key is giving yourself credit for what you did get done and not kicking yourself for what you didn't. You made the bed? Badass. You didn't fold the laundry. Equally badass. Because I know you. You used your badass time and your badass self to do other badass shit that you decided to do.

And a badass gets things done in her own time. Don't let anyone tell you otherwise. You are amazing, and you are someone who makes things happen. And that is all you really need to know.

Even the things that others may see as weaknesses make up who we are, and owning them is powerful, more powerful than whatever hold—or perceived hold—those weaknesses have on us. For example, I am known to procrastinate. But the fact that I know that to be true and am successful despite it is part of what makes me a badass.

Sure, there are deadlines, appointments, and hard and fast time constraints, and you have to work within such limits. But outside of that, I get to get my work done how and when it works for me, and you should do the same. Give yourself credit and don't let anyone tell you otherwise. If the deadline is Monday at 9:00 and you hit send at 8:59, you met the deadline—period, with no explanations or excuses necessary.

You know yourself. You know your strengths and your weaknesses, and you have the right and the responsibility to honor them—the hard edges, the soft spots, and everything in between. They are all what make you you, and staying true to that is what gives you your power.

It can be easy to let other people's judgments or rejection make you feel like less of a badass.

It can be easy to let insecurity about work make you feel like less of a badass. That's certainly understandable, but it doesn't have to be that way. If you are confronted by those feelings, follow my dad's advice—thank your brain for the awareness and let it go. Those feelings don't serve you, so there's no need to hang onto them.

You are not a badass *in spite* of who you are. You are a badass *because* of who you are. You are a badass because you *know* who you are. And if that feels like something you're not 100 percent sure of right this moment, then let's use this very time and space to take stock. Here's a little quiz that can help guide your inquiry.

Where do you feel most yourself?

With whom do you feel most yourself?

When do you feel most yourself?

In what attire do you feel most yourself?

What do you feel most yourself eating?

What do you feel most yourself doing: Listening to music or a podcast? Watching TV or a movie?

What kind of work makes you feel most yourself?

What kind of hobbies or activities make you feel most yourself?

Think of the times that you felt—

> the most whole
> the happiest
> the most relaxed
> the most relieved
> the most proud
> the most accomplished
> the most successful
> the kindest
> the funniest

Using your answers as a guide, take stock of where your true center lies. Knowing that can really help you to manifest your badass self and your badass life. Think of this book as your toolbox, one that you can return to again and again. If you are ever feeling less than centered, come back and quiz yourself again. There's nothing wrong with recalibrating. Medical equipment, appliances—all kinds of things have to be recalibrated. Nothing wrong with doing that for ourselves.

Finding out who we are is a lifelong journey. At our core, we know. But that doesn't mean we shouldn't keep searching and exploring. Fifteen years ago, I really believed I was the girl who sat on the bench

and held the coats while everyone else went on the
roller coaster, hiked the trail, biked the mountain,
or rode the horses. I was scared of everything, so
I defined myself as the one who watched, or kept
score, or protected the belongings.

But I had an *aha* moment on one trip to Disney
World. I was about to leave the line for the Splash
Mountain ride (which is no more) at the "point of no
return," having waited in line with my daughter and
my girlfriend at the time for as long as was allowed
for non-riders.

They begged me to come on the ride with them,
and as I was protesting, I saw the dreaded "mom"
bench out of the corner of my eye. It was filled with
exhausted moms covered in spilled drinks, discarded
snacks, and weepy children. I looked back at all of
the people in line so excited to ride, and I thought,
"This is your life, Jenny Block. Where do you want to
live? On the rides or the benches?"

So, I went on that ride. I didn't love it or hate it.
But I did love that I overcame a lifelong fear and
learned a truth about myself: I am someone who
can do anything despite being scared. The world
has opened up in the most dramatic way since then.
Saying yes to Splash Mountain led to the Year of
Yes, and after that, the Life of Yes. If an opportunity

presents itself, I don't let my fear or how I've defined myself in the past stop me.

You know who you are.

You are not your job.

You are not your partner.

You are not your family.

You are not your failures.

You are not your yeses or your noes.

You are you.

You are a badass.

You know yourself.

Loud and proud—

I am a badass.

I know myself.

Yes! You do!

Manifesting Moments

"I didn't believe that manifesting was a real thing until I read a book about twenty years ago, I don't quite recall the title. The author talked about how she manifested a cubic yard of rich compost. As in, she literally manifested it out of thin air. She was surprised and amazed.

I've never manifested something as definite and physical as that, but I've played around with trying out specific small things. Like during the summer I had breast cancer and subsequently had several lymph nodes removed from my right armpit, and then learned about lymphedema; I was concerned about getting mosquito bites on my right arm, which could trigger lymphedema swelling.

I spent time sitting in my 'Back Forty,' and I 'spoke' to the mosquitoes there. I told them that I understood that they needed blood, so they had my permission to bite my left arm or either leg, but not my right arm. I did not get any mosquito bites on my right arm that entire summer. The mosquitoes seemed to comply with my request, even when I was away from my property.

I also participate in an annual New Year's tradition of setting intentions for the year, which I do with a little online group. This year I wanted "more time"—more time to read, relax, and be creative. I laughed out loud when I looked at my vision board a few months later and realized that having extended time off for my foot surgery had certainly given me more time. And now I'll be having surgery again in early December. The universe is reminding me to be careful what I wish for!"

—Kaye H., Fern Festie

"For me, manifesting means thinking or envisioning change; setting goals and then achieving those goals. I can't say for certain whether it was manifestation or just good old hardheadedness that propelled me to completely change the course of my life two different times, and who knows what could happen next? (Just kidding!) I manifested a new life when I divorced my husband, with three kids and no full-time job. I knew I could have a better life and be happy, and I did it! Completely walked away from the life we had to start a new one. I believe we have the power to manifest both good and bad in our lives. If a person thinks negatively, life will be negative and vice versa."

—Deb Denny, financial advisor

"I believe your thoughts can manifest what happens in your life. People will themselves to be sick or to be well. You can manifest a successful life with your thinking; I also think that people can manifest a negative life."

—Shell Kennedy, Kennedy A Plus Builders

"Manifesting to me is a knowing that what is supposed to happen for me will happen for me as long as I put in the work. By putting in the work, I mean personally, professionally, and spiritually— as a wife, mother, and friend, and in all the other aspects of my life. I have always believed that the worst answer anyone could ever tell me would be 'no.' But even if someone did tell me 'no,' I would still be standing in exactly the same place as I was before I asked the question. Nothing ventured, nothing gained."

—Emily Kaufman, "Travel Mom" and TV personality

CHAPTER FIVE

~~~~~~~~~

WHEN YOU LIFT OTHERS UP, YOU LIFT YOURSELF UP TOO

If You Can Support Someone Else in Their Journey, You Will Find Yourself Supported as Well

It's an amazing thing. When you help someone else, you begin to create a web of support; first one person, then another, then another. And each person you help then becomes a part of a group ready to help you. You lift them up, and they in turn lift you up. And it's not a quid pro quo, it's not something you should expect. Not everyone understands this, but your herd will know, and that's how you will know they are your herd. Lift yourself up by lifting up others. There's no prize for being an island!

I am a badass.

I lift up other badasses.

What makes me feel badass today?

I am a badass.

I lift up other badasses.

What fear will I face today?

I am a badass.

I lift up other badasses.

What can I do today to make me feel even more badass?

I am a badass.

I lift up other badasses.

What fellow badass can I connect with today?

I am a badass.

I lift up other badasses.

Why is being a badass important to me?

I am a badass.

I lift up other badasses.

Badasses always support other badasses. Supporting other badasses does not take away from my badassery. It took me longer than it should have to fully embrace that sentiment and let it permeate through all I am and do. I'm there now, 97 percent anyway, but for a long time, there was one person in particular with whom I just could not seem to get there.

This is one of those sad stories that luckily has a very happy ending. I lived in Dallas, Texas, for a very long time. I was doing lots of food and entertainment writing when I lived there, and I was going to lots of events like restaurant openings, press dinners, shows, and concerts.

Before long, you begin to recognize a regular cast of characters at these events for media and VIPs. As with anything in life, there are people you're excited to see, people who you wish you didn't have to see, and people you don't know and then, for me, there was Rachel.

She seemed to know everyone and everyone seemed to know her. She was pretty and smart and nice and funny—very funny. I wanted to be her. Whew. It feels good admitting that in writing even though those feelings were from so long ago. (A badass admits her feelings even when they aren't her favorite kind. Why? Because you can't manifest the things you want until you make room for them by putting down regrets you've been carrying.)

Wasting energy on envy and hate and self-pity kills good manifesting energy.

Which brings me back to Rachel, who seemed to have manifested it all. And by all, I mean all of things I wanted to be. Pretty, smart, funny, adored, and, most of all, successful and recognized in this highly competitive world of writing. So I did what any girl does when filled with envy: I smiled and waved and stayed ten feet away.

She never approached me. I never approached her. We kept our distance, and I convinced myself that she was way too good for the likes of me with her zillions of followers and invitations and adoring fans. And then one day, years later, fate brought us together, right next to one another, actually.

I was in Portland, Oregon, to cover my favorite annual food festival, Feast Portland. It became a pilgrimage of sorts for me; I would go every year and see the same chefs and colleagues and guests, and meet lots of new folks. Sadly, it is now defunct.

I would be gone for a week, traveling in the area to learn more about the Oregon food scene, and then back in Portland for the dinners and tastings and parties. One year, I got in line to enter the main festival and before I knew it, there she was standing right in front of me. People were already gathering behind me. There was nowhere to go, not gracefully anyway.

I saw her. She saw me. She saw me see her. I saw her
see me. You get the idea. "Hey, how are you?" I said.
"Good. How are you?" she replied. "I don't know
if we've ever met formally. I'm Jenny Block." She
laughed. "I know who you are. I'm Rachel..." "I know
who you are," I interrupted.

She asked if I had ever been to Feast before and I
told her I had, every year other than the first. "How
about you?" I asked. She told me this was her first.
"It the best food festival in the country. Hands
down," I told her. "Okay!" she said.

Well, it went something like that. What I remember
viscerally though is the feeling of being around her.
I got it. She was warm and inviting and familiar
honestly. I soon found out that she too is Jewish.
Both married. Both moms. Both writers. Both living
in the same city. And—best of all—both have the
same sense of humor. We were inseparable for the
rest of the festival.

"How have we never..." I asked her the next day.
"I didn't think you..." she interrupted me. "Well, I
didn't think you..." I in turn broke in.

We both had the same fears about one another, that
the other was too "fancy" for the likes of us. And, if
I'm being really honest, I felt like I *needed* to dislike
her or at least steer clear of her because there wasn't

room in this town for the both of us. I couldn't have been any more wrong on any more levels.

That weekend we had so much fun together, and, more importantly, we have been best friends ever since. I moved away from Dallas not long after that, which was incredibly sad. I only live three hours away. But still, we wasted more than fifteen years of potential friendship avoiding each other. I try not to waste too much time mourning the loss and instead use it as a lesson that has served me well on my manifesting journey.

I am better when she is better. I am uplifted when she is uplifting. Supporting her doesn't take away from me. Sure, there are only so many writing gigs and opportunities, but even if she gets something that maybe I could have, it wasn't meant for me. She is manifesting her own badass life. And her success is in no way a roadblock to me. It makes me so happy when she has a success that it fills me in some ways that even my own success cannot.

That's my girl! I think. *Look at her go!*

We have traveled all over together. Eaten a million things together. Met the most interesting people together. She has edited stories and books, including this one, for me and a book for my dad too. She is always there when I need to be reminded that I am

The Little Engine That Could, even when I feel like anything but.

So, now, when I walk in somewhere and there's someone who seems too "fancy" for me, I make a beeline for them. I introduce myself, and—nine times out of ten—I end up connecting with them. And when we make that connection, I feel propelled by their success, joy, and magnetism.

It's tricky, I get it. The world can be a competitive place. But here's the thing: if you are manifesting a badass life for your badass self, you need to be surrounded by badass energy, not wasting your time and power pushing it away. Badass energy begets badass energy. It may not be a law in physics, but it is definitely a law of badassery.

Ok, okay. I hear you. I hear that inner critic making you think, "It's too scary." "What if they reject me?" "Who am I to be bothering them?" "I don't need anyone else." "I am having enough trouble being supportive to myself, let alone anyone else."

Well, most things worth doing are scary at first. Who cares? You're a badass. No one is an island. You get what you give.

Sure, it might be a little bit scary, but it's not a pit of snakes, it's a "hello" and a handshake. Even if you hate it, you can do it. It's a split second that holds a world of possibilities.

And so what if they reject you? I mean, the worst that could happen is that they say "hello" back and then turn away. Fine. On to the next. Truth be told, they may be either rude, unkind, preoccupied, or scared of you. Regardless of which it is, you don't need any of that, so it's no big loss—no loss at all, really.

You are you, and you are amazing. You can keep reading that as many times as you need to. You are a badass, and that's enough. You are worthy, certainly worthy of introducing yourself to anyone you like.

You do need other people—you do. Very few things by very few people are done totally alone. And there's no need to go it alone. Part of being a badass is manifesting the people you want and need around you. So, for goodness' sake, say, "Hello!"

Allow me to let you in on a little secret: supporting other people is a means of supporting yourself. Go ahead, read that again if you like; it only gets more true. When you support others, you prove to yourself that you are capable of doing that. And if you can do it for someone else, you can do it for yourself, too.

The world can be a tough place. It can be fast, competitive, and even mean. But your little corner of it doesn't have to be. You get to manifest that circle of support around you. That means you get to create it.

Here are some real world steps to making this happen:

1. Put yourself in the places where the people are. Like the Little Mermaid, you might need to acquire the thing that gives you entrée to those places and groups and events. Hopefully you won't have to sell your soul to a sea witch or anything. But you may need to take up that activity you've been thinking about doing. Want to hang out with people who knit? Grab some needles. People who skateboard? Get thee to the skate shop. People who love movies? Set up some films and get watching.

2. Get in the mix. You can perhaps lurk at the start, be it online or in real life. But, at some point, you have to jump in. Come with a question. Answer a question that's been posed. Join a conversation. Let people know you want to join in. All too often, we discover too late that people were respecting our privacy, not ignoring us. So preempt the problem and step in. Step into your badass life.

3. Keep going. Maybe you don't find your herd the first time out of the gate. Maybe it was

the wrong gate. Are you being honest with yourself about who you want to surround yourself with? Don't think, "Who *should I want* to be around?" Think, "Who *do I want* to be around?" In other words, maybe you want to be an influencer. Do you have to hang out with other influencers? Not if the desire to support them doesn't well up in you when you meet them, and not if they don't seem to offer the kind of support you need. Hang out with the people connected to the areas of life for which you want to be an influencer. Take a cooking class. Join the roller derby team. Go thrifting. Renovate a brownstone. Take up foraging. You get the idea!

I know you know what I'm saying here, but I'm going to say it one more time: Supporting others supports you. It's as simple as that. So don't be afraid to meet the people you admire, the people already doing it, the people you want to be. Walk into those circles, and walk into your power and your manifesting. Your badass life awaits.

Remember, most regret ends up being about the things we didn't do, not the things we did.

You are a badass.

You lift up other badasses.

Your turn—

I am a badass.

I lift up other badasses.

You sure do! Every day!

Manifesting Moments

" 'To manifest' can imply creating something out of nothing, which can sound really magical or ethereal, and that's *great*! But I'm a pragmatist in life, so I don't believe in leaving everything to chance.

To me, 'manifesting' something—whether it's a relationship, success in a business venture, a level of financial comfort, or a life experience from your list of 'Things to See Before I Die'—is putting a situation in motion that wasn't just going to happen on its own. I believe the act of creation involves first speaking the idea into existence, the mere speaking of which may bring something seemingly impossible into the realm of the attainable.

Take your pick of any of these things that did not exist, but were spoken into reality:

'We choose to go to the moon in this decade and do the other things, not because they are easy, but because they are hard,' declared John F. Kennedy in 1962, speaking of a goal which became a reality in 1969.

Martin Luther King Jr. affirmed in 1963 when he said he had a dream that one day this nation would rise up and live out the true meaning of its creed: 'We hold these truths to be self-evident, that all men are created equal.'

Doctors speak of 'manifesting a cure.' The cures to diseases were not going to happen by themselves until someone spoke that cure into existence. Smallpox was eradicated and there are still teams of researchers working on other conditions including HIV/AIDS, cancer, Alzheimer's, heart disease, and diabetes.

I could say 'I'm going to be in a successful relationship' by a certain date or 'I'm going to be debt-free.'

Then, the pragmatist in me makes lists: What steps need to happen between *now* and the situation I'm manifesting to bring it into reality? I make a list, breaking it down into manageable milestones with measurable results. After following those steps, that which was previously thought to be unlikely or even impossible may be my new reality. Was it mystical and ethereal or a combination of an intention, an utterance, and action? Take your pick. Anything is possible!"

—Eric Ross Allen, Eric Allen Productions

CHAPTER SIX

~~~~~~

YOU HAVE A RIGHT TO EVERYTHING YOU ARE AND EVERYTHING YOU HAVE

When I Achieve Something, It's Because I Deserve to Achieve It

Don't let anyone steal your joy and don't let anyone tell you it's all luck, or that it was all due to some favor from someone, or that someone other than you should have what you have. You did this. You created this. You have this. The present is yours. The future is yours. And it's all because of how deserving and focused you are. It's because you are you, and you make your visions a reality. Jealous people like to steal other people's thunder. Don't let them have it!

I am a badass.

I am worthy.

What makes me feel badass today?

I am a badass.

I am worthy.

What fear will I face today?

I am a badass.

I am worthy.

What can I do today to make me feel even more badass?

I am a badass.

I am worthy.

What fellow badass can I connect with today?

I am a badass.

I am worthy.

Why is being a badass important to me?

I am a badass.

I am worthy.

Half the time, I feel like I deserve more. The other half of the time, I feel like I don't deserve what I have. The key is finding a balance. You get what you put out there. And when you get back the love, success, and joy, you can say, "I did that!"

When my first book came out in 2008, my publisher
nominated me for a Lambda Literary Award. I was so
excited when I made the finalist list and decided to
go to New York City for the awards ceremony. But
as soon as I got there, I just felt like a total fraud. I
imagined everyone else thinking, "What's she doing
here? She's never going to win!" I was a horrible
grump all day. My girlfriend at the time was with me
and did her best to cheer me up.

"You've been nominated for a big award!" she said.
"I don't know why," I told her, attitude fully on lock.
"Because you're a great writer! Come on, this should
be fun!" she said. But I simply couldn't hear it. "It's
stupid. I'm not going to win. And how embarrassing
that I flew out here just to make a fool of myself
acting like a real writer. Did you see the other people
who were nominated? What was I thinking?"

"You were thinking, they nominated me, so I will go.
And here we are. In New York City. Even if you don't
win…" she said. "So you don't think I'm going to win.
I knew it," I said, stomping into the other room. She
tried again, "No, no, no. That's not what I meant. I
just meant…" "Whatever," I said.

I took a shower. But I refused to wash my hair. We
were almost late. I insisted on sitting in the back
so I could slink away quietly when I lost, but then I
heard, "The winner is…Jenny Block!" I was frozen. I

was sure I had heard wrong. I didn't move from my seat. People were clapping and cheering and looking around for me.

My girlfriend nudged me excitedly, "That's you!" Somehow I made it to the front of the room.

"I'm sorry that took me so long. I'm wearing my big girl shoes tonight," I said, modeling my shoes. Everyone laughed, and somehow I gave a quick thank you speech even though I had nothing prepared because I wasn't going to win since I was nothing but a big fraud and they all knew it.

Except no one thought that.

I'm not a fraud. I am worthy. I am worthy of an award and success and love. I nearly ruined an amazing night in the arc of my life. And as much as I try to avoid regret, I do regret how I behaved that day. Let this be a public apology to my girlfriend at the time, who always believed in me, especially when I didn't.

I'd love to tell you that was the only time I've felt that way. But that would be a lie, and I promised to be honest with you. I mean, how could you trust the process if you don't trust me to tell the truth?

So, I'll tell you my truth. Impostor syndrome still pops up every once in a while. But now, when it sneaks up, I do my best to remind myself that those feelings are unwarranted and that feeling them doesn't serve me, it only hurts me.

To heal this, we have to get to the bottom of it. This is necessary because, like so many other issues, wasting our energy on impostor syndrome takes away the power we should be putting toward manifesting the badass lives we want. So much of the success of manifesting depends on putting your energy in the right places and not wasting it in the wrong ones. And feeling like a fraud is definitely a waste.

I think for me, impostor syndrome has to do with wrestling with the meaning of success. I have never made a lot of money. But I have had incredible opportunities, and I have accomplished some pretty incredible things.

At the time of writing this book, I am a regular contributor to the *New York Times* and have been for nearly five years. I started writing about weddings, and now I dabble in fashion too. This is my fifth book. I have traveled all around the world. I have interviewed celebrities. I've gone to the Formula 1 races in Monza. I've rappelled down the side of an eighteen-story hotel. I've slept on the Great Barrier Reef in Australia.

I'm not a fraud.

But perhaps because the world judges us on looks, money, and celebrity, my brain continues to argue with me. "You're not a supermodel." "You don't make a zillion dollars." "You don't need a bodyguard to walk you down the street."

But the brain needs to keep its big mouth shut. It doesn't know what it's talking about! I get to decide what success means, and by my own account, I'm doing pretty darn okay.

The you that you were five years ago wishes she had what you have today.

That's another mantra I have added to my collection. It's so true. It's all about perspective—a badass knows that when she isn't feeling quite so badass, it's usually because she's lost perspective.

Social media is the worst when it comes to maintaining perspective. It can make you think you are doing it all wrong. It can leave you questioning everything from your work to your body, from your friends to your family to your bank account. But social media can also be a godsend if you look at it with your eyes open.

Remind yourself that what you see is highly curated and designed to do exactly what it's doing—making you feel like you need to be someone different than you are. Most of what you see is either faked, filtered, or far-fetched. Use social media for fun. But don't use it as a measuring stick.

Now, you can use your own social media as an inventory or check-in of sorts. You can use Instagram or even the photos on your phone. When I look back through my Instagram feed or flick thought the albums on my phone, I can't help but smile—at all of the places I've gone, people I've spent time with, art I've seen, and adventures I've had. Sometimes I'm surprised—and dare I say even impressed—with what I find there.

I did that. I saw that. I met those people. I manifested all of that joy and light and experience and fun. I did that.

And you do that too—all of the time. You do it because you are worthy of it, worthy of every friend, every trip, and every experience. You are worthy for no reason other than you being you. That is enough. In fact, that is more than enough. That is everything.

Maybe impostor syndrome is there to keep us humble. If so, I get it and I appreciate it. But like my dad says with a lot of things, when it's no longer serving me, I thank it for the reminder that although I am worthy, I am also lucky and grateful and I send it on its way.

Anything that is not serving you while you are manifesting has to be sent on its way. You cannot be wasting time and energy on people and places and things that are not worthy of you, and that is the only issue of worthiness you should be bothering with.

You are worthy of everything. But not everything is worthy of you.

Sadly, some of what might make you feel unworthy could be the people, places, and things that surround you. If there are people who make you feel lousy about yourself, it's time to remove them from your world. If they are people you have to see for one reason or another, limit your time with them, and set boundaries for things you will talk about with them to protect yourself.

Negative energy is a detriment to manifesting, and you need as little of it in your life as possible.

For some people, where they spend their time can have a massive impact on how they feel about themselves. For me, a messy room is a no-go. Even if I have a ton to do, I have to take the time to get my study in order before I can get to work. Or else I relocate to another room in the house. Even if my study is tidy, sometimes I'll move outside or take my puppy for a coffee date at Starbucks and work there.

Environment is important. When I was writing my first book, I would drive all the way from Richmond, Virginia, to Washington, DC, to write at a coffee shop by day/bar by night called Tryst. Being there made me feel like a writer. So, I was a writer. When people asked what I did, I said, "I'm a writer." It was like speaking truth to power: my truth is that I am a writer. The power manifested in my life when the universe heard me say that was *the truth*. The universe's only mission is to love, protect, and help you.

For others, what they wear or how they look helps them to feel worthy. Let me be very clear here, there's no one right way to look or be. The point is that feeling your best can help you feel worthy. When I'm feeling less than, I eat food that makes my body feel good. I get out and move, whether it's a stroll through my neighborhood, a dance party for one, or a session of *qigong*. I put something on that makes me feel great, a pretty sundress, a comfy hoodie, or an over-the-top look. Whatever makes me feel my best at the moment makes me feel worthy of that moment.

Now let's talk people. If you are trying to make something happen for yourself, you need to surround yourself with people who want that for you as well. Maybe it's people who are literally helping by editing pages you wrote, packing boxes, throwing practice pitches, or managing your social media outreach. Or maybe it's simply people who say, "You've got this!" "Go for it!" "You deserve that!" "Good for you!" "I knew you could do it!"

What you cannot have are people who undermine you. Even though it's likely that their lack of support is 100 percent about them, it's still hurtful at worst and unhelpful at best. So, if the people in your household or your current circle at not doing it for you, get out there and find your herd.

Join groups, online and in real life. Talk to people. Go to events. Attend conferences. Try out classes or workshops or meet-ups. Heck, go to the dog park if that's where you run into that one woman who always asks what you're up to and is truly excited to hear all about it.

You are worthy. That's not in question. Impostor syndrome is real. Wishing it away is not the answer.

Make choices that make you feel worthy—that's
how you get to the good stuff. Badass manifesting
is all about moving through the world in a way that
best serves where you want to be in life.

You are a badass.

You are worthy.

Say it with me now—

I am a badass.

I am worthy.

Yes you are!

Manifesting Moments

"I really like the idea of manifesting, and to me it means something like calling up your destiny—calling it into existence or actuality. In many ways, I feel that I manifested my husband Aaron. I had always seen dating as like a punchline—it was all just material for stand-up, almost. I dated men who weren't appropriate partners. Then slowly I started moving away from that—I split off from a bad guy who it felt like had me under mind control for four years. I dated a guy who was a more appropriate match. It didn't work out, and that breakup was *very* painful, but I *do* feel like it put me in a place to be ready for Aaron—ready for *real* love and total honesty."

—Selena Coppock, editorial director, *Princeton Review*, former stand-up comedian, creator of IG @NYTVows, and former cohost of the *Betches Brides* podcast

"Manifestation is to me the act of channeling my thoughts and desires into the universe, inviting divine intelligence to guide the way. I believe in the power of intention to shape reality, and I have seen this play out time and again in both my career and my personal life: from the moment I read about NASA divers and knew that was my calling, to my sixteen years at BP, where each role I have felt destined for has become mine through the focused energy of manifestation. The same instinct led me to my wife; the moment we met, I knew. Now, five years later, we have an incredible daughter and a life built on those intuitions made real."

—Virginia Moore, dream weaver extraordinaire

"It's like believing a goal into reality. Having a good positive attitude will lead to success."

—Brooke Thomas, teacher

"Manifesting means putting out good energy in the universe about something you hope comes true. *Hope* comes to mind when I think of manifesting. I am in a constant state of manifesting; I always believe that I can do what I set out to do, and I don't let any outside factors influence that."

—Tommy DiDario, host of the iHeartMedia podcast *I've Never Said This Before* and entertainment correspondent on Extra TV

"The closest thing to manifestation that I do is intention setting. I think manifestation can be closely aligned to prayer for the agnostic person and feels somewhat passive. In my mind, setting an intention has a similar effect, but it inspires me to action. I have a standing weekly chat with my friend Theresa, who helps ground me in my intentions, so I guess I do this through verbal processing;

but I also occasionally do it through journaling and meditation."

—Justine Li, medical student

CHAPTER SEVEN

YOU GET TO DECIDE WHAT THE BADASS VERSION OF YOU LOOKS LIKE

If You Are Comfortable in Your Own Skin, You Will Always Find Comfort

It's a bit of a conundrum. I want to tell you that looks don't matter—because they don't. Except they do. I mean, they don't make someone a good or a bad person. Caring about appearance doesn't make you any less of a person than someone who doesn't care, and vice versa. But let's face it—many of us care about it, yet for some, caring about it can become a downright distraction. And when that happens, it's time to get rid of the distraction. Badasses are as diverse as the population itself. So you get to decide

what makes you feel like your most badass self,
because the more you do that, the more you free
up your mind for manifesting the badass life that's
waiting out there just for you.

I am a badass.

I decide—for me—what a badass looks like.

What makes me feel badass today?

I am a badass.

I decide—for me—what a badass looks like.

What fear will I face today?

I am a badass.

I decide—for me—what a badass looks like.

What can I do today to make me feel even
more badass?

I am a badass.

I decide—for me—what a badass looks like.

What fellow badass can I connect with today?

I am a badass.

I decide—for me—what a badass looks like.

Why is being a badass important to me?

I am a badass.

I decide—for me—what a badass looks like.

I am what a badass looks like because I am a badass. I decide what I want to look like, and I will do and wear what makes me feel the most like me.

I feel compelled to share this story because it seems to me that a lot of people who struggle with their badassery also struggle with how they look. I think there's a myth that if you really are a badass, you love yourself just the way you are, and I think that's a load of bunk.

If you do, great! If you don't, well, that's okay too. And if you want to change something, you have every right to do that. Here's the thing, being a badass is only dependent on one thing—you feeling like one. So, if looking a certain way makes you feel like a badass, have at it.

For me, that meant plastic surgery. People often comment that I must be obsessed with my looks to go so far as to go under the knife. But in what is perhaps an ironic twist, the more I have done, the less I have thought about it. Why? Because the problem I saw was fixed and I didn't need to think about it anymore.

"But we gave you that nose," I remember my parents saying in unison, as if it had been some treasured gift bought and paid for with their hard-earned money when I called the night before I had my nose job. It wasn't that I hadn't tried to tell them sooner. I tried. I tried hard.

But every time I brought it up, either my mother or my father would change the subject. "Hi, mom," I'd say. "Hi, how are you?" she'd ask her. I'd tell her I was doing great and ask how she was.

"I'm good," she'd say. "What's up?" I'd take a deep breath. "Well, I've decided to get a nose job." The line would fall silent, and then my mother would say, "How's the weather in Richmond?" That was how the conversations went, starting at about six months out then.

But it was indiscernible from all of the identical conversations that would follow. They just would not talk about it. It wasn't like it was an entirely new subject. I had wanted to hack off that offensive appendage for years. It was the one gift I'd wanted for my sixteenth birthday.

"Please," I had begged. "Absolutely not," my mom had said, "It's ridiculous." I balled my fists and could feel my face turning red. "Maybe for you. But look at me," I said to her. She told me I was beautiful, and I reminded her that she was just saying that because she was my mom. "I would feel that way even if I wasn't your mother." I pleaded,

"Moooooooooommmmm." But all she said
was, ""No."

My sweet sixteen was quite an affair. Everything
was pink: streamers, plates, cups, napkins, and
plasticware. But my dress was red—the effect was
very dramatic. I loved the contrast, as well as the
symbolism I imagined, fueled by the interpretations
of novels and poems I was studying in school.

There was a five-foot-long sub and lots of snacks
and soft drinks. The party was all laid out on my
parents' back deck. The house itself wasn't very
exciting, it was a typical two-story home with
three bedrooms and two and a half baths. It had
a brick face and cream shutters. But the deck was
magnificent. My father had built it himself far above
our large, sloping backyard.

From the deck, you had a perfect view of the
neighborhood, with a lake, fields, and trees. And
standing out on that redwood deck, I still had high
hopes that my ultimate teenage wish would come
true despite the fact that my mother had refused my
repeated requests.

Very few people showed up. July birthdays are
hard, my mother would tell me. People are on
vacation, and there is never a good weekend. I was
so disappointed. Although there had only been a few

RSVPs, my mother had assured me there would still be plenty of people there.

But those who did come seemed to be having a good time. We ate off the tentative paper plates and drank from the sweating, pink, plastic cups.

"So, do you think your parents will let you?" my friend Wendy asked me. "I don't know," I replied, "I hope so." Finally it came time to open my presents, my mother handed me a tiny box wrapped in gold foil paper. "We love you," she whispered to me, kissing me on the forehead.

I was holding my breath as I unwrapped the box, hoping a tiny note was nestled inside that just read "Yes." But as soon as I snapped open the hinge of the black velvet box, my heart sank. A lovely pair of the teeniest diamond stud earrings was nestled within the silk.

"Thank you," I managed, choking back tears that I hoped everyone would read as overwhelming gratitude rather than sheer disappointment. I knew my mother knew the truth. I saw those earrings as a garish billboard which cried, "You are an ugly, big-nosed girl, and you will always be one."

Whenever I met someone new, I always made sure to make a crack about my nose right off the bat in an

effort to preempt him or her from making one either
in front of me or behind my back. At stoplights, I
would fidget mercilessly. I would never want anyone
along the road to have a chance to gaze at my
profile. In dressing rooms with three-way mirrors, I
would cover part of my nose with my finger, imaging
what I'd look like sans the Rocky Mountains.

So, when I was a junior in college, I finally had the
surgery. "Rhino septoplasty" was how it appeared
on the receipt from the credit card I had gotten at
school from some guy who was giving away free
water bottles with every sign-up.

I had it done over spring break. When I got back,
there were all sorts of questions—but none of the
ones I expected. "Did you get a haircut?" "You look
different. Tanner? Thinner?" "Wow. Did you get
contacts?" I didn't even wear glasses.

In the week we were out of school, I had the surgery
and fully recovered. The first few weeks, I couldn't
stop checking out my profile in every mirror,
window, and reflection. I had to stop myself from
making big nose jokes because I didn't have one
anymore. Before long, I stopped thinking about my
nose altogether.

I don't know if they really were easier or not, but
things seemed easier after that. People seemed

kinder and flirtier. Here's a little secret though:
It wasn't them, it was me. I acted differently
because I felt differently, so people responded to
me differently.

In doing so, I manifested feeling confident about the
way I look.

I've had a series of ups and downs on that front,
times when I just didn't feel like I looked the part of
the badass, and that made it nearly impossible for
me to be a badass, at least in my own mind. And let
me take a minute to say that how you feel in your
mind is really important. In fact, it just might be the
most important thing of all when it comes to your
badass journey.

Don't let people make you feel bad about feeling
bad. That's a real thing. And it can stop you from
being who you really are and getting what you really
want. So, acknowledge the feeling and seek a way to
resolve it.

And for anyone out there saying, "If you're a real
badass, you wouldn't care how you look or what
other people think," to them I would say, "If you
don't care how you look or what other people
think, that's great. But if we're being honest with
ourselves, most of us do."

You need to feel like your badass self, whatever that means. Therefore, if making changes will make you feel powerful, then go for it! Think about it; "badass" looks so different depending on the world you move through. And if you feel like a part of that world, you feel like more of a badass.

Nothing makes me more insecure than sticking out like a sore thumb. Call me what you want, but that's my truth. I don't want to be the girl who's underdressed for a party. But I never mind going a little over-the-top. Maybe the opposite is true for you. Maybe you want to be the mysterious one all in black so that no one is sure whether or not they even saw you at the event.

All I know is that when the image in my head of what badass me looks like matches my reality, I can do ten times more than when it doesn't. When I go to a party, a wedding, or anywhere there's going to be dancing, I wear dancing clothes and shoes. I don't feel confident dancing in flats or in something overly tight or stuffy. I just don't. I don't know why, I just know it's true.

So, don't judge people who want to make changes, especially if that's coming from wishing you could make those changes too! And don't judge yourself either. Badass you looks however you define your badass look. And if your badass meter is running low, think about whether it might be because you aren't seeing the most badass version of yourself when you look in the mirror.

Maybe it's time to retire that old T-shirt. Maybe it's time for a new hairdresser. Perhaps an at-home spa day with hair and skin masks and a DIY manicure will do the trick. Heck, maybe you need a nap and a walk around the block to get some Vitamin D and put some color in your cheeks.

It's okay. It's okay not to love the way you look and it's okay to make the changes you want to make. And it's okay to not be okay with, "You look fine. Who cares?" You care, and that's all that matters.

Now, I have one caveat for you, and it's a biggie. Do not expect—or demand—that anyone else think a certain way about the changes you make or the results of those changes. People can say what they want—and they will. This is about you and only you. If you don't feel badass, do what makes you feel badass.

Join that gym. Buy that hot pink fringe jacket. Pull out those old jeans that you love. Go back to being a brunette. And before any "body positivity" or "anti-plastic surgery" or "dress your age" advocates come after me, please take a beat and remember: I am not making anyone do anything. And I am not stopping anyone from doing anything. You do you, my friend. And just like you want permission to love yourself as you are, so do my fellow badasses here. Let's not rain on anyone's parade.

There's enough negativity already. I am down for some universal positivity. You don't dig Post Malone's face tattoos and *blingu* teeth? I do. And what is of the only real importance is that *he* does. If you don't like that look, don't get yourself face tattoos and a grill—and don't look down on someone else who made that choice.

A badass needs all of her focus to manifest her badass life. A badass has no time to waste on judging other people or being weighed down by other people's judgment.

Be free, my fellow badasses! Be you! Make the change you want to see that will allow you to manifest your badass self.

You are a badass.

You decide—for you—what a badass looks like.

All together now:

I am a badass.

I decide—for me—what a badass looks like.

Yeah, you are! Just look at you!

Manifesting Moments

"The concept of manifestation as I see it brings up intention, will, and sort of the mysterious workings of the universe. Not to veer too far into the spiritual (I believe in science!), but I also believe there's so much power in belief. As the saying goes, 'Thoughts are things.' Our very thoughts have power over us. We are what we think, if you will. What we give our energy to matters.

I think I've come to believe that if we're being true to ourselves, focusing on goals that align with that—and with a little luck—the universe wants to conspire in our favor.

And I often think about how I manifested my life in New York City. Growing up, I was consumed by television, watching literally hours a day. Countless shows and movies were set here, and I'd dream of living in this magical place—far from the dirty, dysfunctional home I had as a kid. When I began my TV news career in small-town Texas, that dream expanded to include working as a network correspondent in New York City.

There were so many twists and turns. I landed a great job as an anchor in Houston, which is another massive, vibrant city. I was content, and I thought

I'd stay there forever. But those NYC dreams I had, first as a grimy little brown kid, and then as a small-town TV reporter, ended up coming true despite virtually no one believing they would.

It took me trying to push through the walls I put up as a kid to start talking about the way I grew up, as well as being more public about being gay and staying open to the possibility of love, for the dreams to come true."

—Steven Romo, anchor/correspondent, NBC News and MSNBC

"I think manifesting is trying to make things happen in your life. However, I do feel like it is misconstrued to be wishful thinking. Manifesting without an action plan most likely isn't going to produce a result."

—Robert Spiegel, production manager & loan officer at The Spiegel Group

CHAPTER EIGHT

YOU GET TO START FRESH EVERY DAY AND LEAVE THE PAST WHERE IT BELONGS

If You Can Let Yesterday Go, You Can Take Advantage of All of Today's Possibilities

Stuff happens, it really does. It happens to all of us. And it's okay. Even if in the moment it doesn't feel okay, it is. It's okay. And that was yesterday and today is today and if you let the past ruin the present, you're giving the bad thing too much power. Sure, you might want to stay in bed and wallow in embarrassment, or even give up. But how will that help you get to where you want to be? Fine; be sad, mad, mortified, or whatever, for a minute, an hour, or even an afternoon. Then make like a certain

Disney Princess and let it go. It's a whole new day, and it's all yours!

> I am a badass. Today is a new badass day.
>
> What makes me feel badass today?
>
> I am a badass. Today is a new badass day.
>
> What fear will I face today?
>
> I am a badass. Today is a new badass day.
>
> What can I do today to make me feel even more badass?
>
> I am a badass. Today is a new badass day.
>
> What fellow badass can I connect with today?
>
> I am a badass. Today is a new badass day.
>
> Why is being a badass important to me?
>
> I am a badass. Today is a new badass day.

Just because yesterday sucked doesn't mean today will. I have the power to decide what today looks like.

That means I will do badass stuff no matter what yesterday looked like. Listen, we all have shitty days, badasses included. The magic is in how you handle that fact. A badass doesn't let today be ruined by yesterday's failures, disappointments, or misses. This isn't always easy, but it is a badass golden rule. Don't let yesterday ruin your today!

Yesterday is a metaphor, of course. Your yesterday might be a month or a year, or it might even feel like a lifetime. When it comes to past decisions, mistakes, or traumas, sometimes it feels pointless to go on under the weight of the past. "If that's my past, why bother with the future?"

The answer is in the question. Don't give up on what comes next, because what happened before is *in the past*. You have nothing to bother with but the future. We have to accept what was. But that can't stop us from what can be. I've made some major mistakes in my life, ones that could have been deadly—figuratively or literally. The only thing that saved me was knowing that I could leave the past in the past.

I have dated people who were a terrible idea. I have worked jobs I was terrible at and loathed. I have sent out a zillion pitches and gotten back the exact same number of no's. I have bombed on stage—forgetting the words to a song once, the choreography another time, and flat-out choosing the wrong material to perform on yet another occasion.

Each time I did these unfortunate things, I wanted to crawl in a hole and never come out. I wanted the ground to open up and swallow me whole. I wanted the world to stop spinning so I could get off. It seemed like my whole world was over. It seemed like the whole world was over. I figured no one would ever date me again or say yes to a story I wrote again or invite me to perform again.

But the badass in me reminded the scaredy-cat that those are just singular moments on what is hopefully a very long journey. And to throw it all away because today was a wash would be crazy at best and unforgivable at worst. Because the one way to guarantee failure is by giving up. You will definitely fail to get what you want if you never try.

So, if you dig guarantees, there's a crummy one for you.

And, I hate to be overdramatic. I am speaking from experience. There have been a couple of incidents from which I thought I would never recover.

I am a bit of a Girl Scout; I like my chart to be filled with gold stars. So certain things can really knock me back. For example, years ago, I used to write test banks, workbooks, and study guides to go along with textbooks. I was a college English professor, so it was a great fit for me. Usually.

But one project I was working on kept getting sent back to me over and over by the editor. I would apologize and try again, and then I'd apologize and try *again*—over and over. Finally, the editor very nicely told me, "I'm sorry. I just don't think you're a good fit for this project. Looking forward to finding something different for you down the road!"

But what I heard was. "You are so stupid. You can't do anything right. Why did you waste so much of my time? Please go crawl under a rock, and don't try to do anything ever again."

That may sound over the top, but it's true: That's the way I heard it internally. I bawled my eyes out, and I felt like a total idiot. That gig had been right up my alley. How on Earth could I have effed it up?

Then, the next morning, while I was still busy beating myself up, my doorbell rang. It was a flower delivery from my editor. The note with the bouquet read, "At least you didn't get hit in the face with a goose!" Just that week, when the movie star Fabio was riding on a roller coaster, he was hit right in the face by a goose flying through the air. In the aftermath, he said the goose had hit a video camera and broken it, and then a piece of that had cut him. But the tape of the incident was "lost," so we'll never really know.

All we do know is that Fabio's face was bloodied—and that my editor was right: that was much, much, *much* worse! I suddenly could not stop myself from laughing despite my red puffy eyes and exhaustion from tossing and turning in bed all night, trying to figure out why I was such a dummy.

I went back and looked at her email again. "I'm sorry. I just don't think you're a good fit for this project. Looking forward to finding something different for you down the road!" When I read it with fresh, albeit red, eyes, I saw that she'd apologized and she wanted to work with me again! She didn't see me as the problem, but instead thought the match between me and that particular assignment was the problem.

After a hot shower and a lot more giggling, I got myself together, forgave myself both for losing the gig and for my response to losing the gig, and moved on. It was a new badass day and it was laid out ahead of me for the taking. That all sounds very simple in retrospect. But it wasn't easy to move forward and that is something I continue to work on.

Every day is a new day to walk away from the things that didn't and don't serve you and walk toward the things that do.

Another time an editor called me out for doing something out of turn that I didn't even do. And once a PR company blasted me for something an editor added to one of my stories that I didn't know about. Then there was that fateful day in the school gym back when I was in the seventh grade.

My best friend at the time was a champion roller skater. And, yes, that is a thing, at least, it was a thing in the 80s. Anyway, she was a rock star, and she was my best friend. So, when she was going to do a skating demonstration at school one day, I got to introduce her. The whole school was there sitting in the stands as I started walking to the center of the floor.

I was smiling and waving, thinking about what I was going to say. What I was apparently *not* thinking about was watching my step, because just as I got to the center, I tripped. I face-planted in front of the entire school. My life literally flashed before my eyes, and I swear I could hear my father's voice. "Pop on up, kiddo. Nothing to do now but pop on up and keep on smiling."

And that is precisely what I did. I popped up; I smiled. I took a grand, sweeping, ballet style curtsy and waved. Everyone waved back and clapped, I introduced my friend, and that was that.

I wanted to *die*. But afterwards, everyone just laughed with me and said, "Best recovery ever." I was so proud of myself, and I tucked that moment away and have never allowed myself to forget it. Sometimes, it's not even a matter of *tomorrow* is a new *day*. Sometimes, it's as simple as right now is not five minutes ago. It's right now. Whatever just happened just happened. But right now, you have a choice: Lie there on the floor and cry, or take a bow.

Always choose to take a bow.

Here's the thing, the other option is to curl into a ball and stay there. The other option is to believe that since one bad thing happened, everything else that happens is going to be bad. That thinking will get you nowhere—fast. Badass manifesting is all about setting your intentions and keeping your mind and your actions focused on that intention.

The thing is, if you put your focus on failure, you can bet your bottom dollar that failure is precisely what you have coming your way. When someone says, "See! I told you today was going to be terrible," "See! I told you I was going to fail," or "See! I told you I would never get that role/job/opportunity!" they knew it was going to happen ahead of time because they made it happen!

We are far more powerful than we know. And although manifesting is not a wave-your-wand-and-say-the-secret-words kind of magic trick, it is based on mind power. Write the thing down. Say it in your mind. Say it out loud to yourself. Speak it into reality by sharing it with others. Then do the work.

Designer handbags and job offers are not going to drop from the sky. But opportunities that can get you both of those are there for the taking if your intentions are set and your eyes are open. Don't zap your power or thwart your manifesting by worrying about yesterday.

I mean, think about it. Imagine if you started every day with one or all of the mantras in this book. Imagine where your head would be and what you could accomplish with that kind of focus, self-empowerment, and drive.

Yesterday is over. Past failures are just that: in the past. Every day is a new day that is yours for the taking. The only question is—what will you do with these twenty-four precious hours?

You are a badass.

Today is a new badass day.

Say it like you mean it.

I am a badass.

Today is a new badass day.

It most certainly is!

Manifesting Moments

"I want to believe in manifestation, and I do to
an extent. I think we can give power to things—
good and bad—by how much we focus our
attention on them.

Honestly, I wish I believed more. As with all things
that require faith, I think I still have a bad taste in
my mouth from some religious trauma I endured
growing up. I also admit I'm more inclined to believe
things that are measurable and quantifiable.

However, my husband Steven does like to say I
manifested our second dog, Theo. Cu (our first
dog) was saved from what sounded like a pet-
hoarding situation. The other dogs from his litter
were sent to different homes. When I saw a photo
of Theo, though, I wanted him immediately. I saw a
resemblance to Cu, so I thought it would be so great
to have him here with us. We also wanted Cu to have
a companion to help ease his separation anxiety.

But the new family that had taken Theo in didn't
want to give him up. We asked a couple times and
they said no way, they loved him too much. Finally,
months later, their housing situation changed and
they asked if we could still take him in. For a while,
it looked like a lost cause. No one seemed to think

we'd get him, but I kept asking. And now he's part of our family."

—Stephen Morgan, meteorologist and television host

"To me, the word manifesting means 'affirmation of alignment.' It's like the universe is giving me help because I'm in alignment. I have manifested things!—both bad and good. I would say I've manifested things by putting a lot of passionate feeling behind whatever I was intentionally thinking about."

—Aryka Randall, filmmaker and photographer

"For me, manifesting is the ability to take a goal from thought to reality. Some people talk about it as 'putting an idea out into the universe.' I see it more like a verb—something that requires action if you want it accomplished."

—Ashley LeBeuve, architect

"For me, I have to mentally work hard to manifest a positive attitude and be open to good things. I do that all the time, and it works! When I feel down or low energy, it's much easier to manifest things that are not positive, which feeds a vicious cycle or spiral. Bottom line, my internal energy or innate wherewithal has a lot to do with what I can manifest. Self-care is key."

—Frannie Apistolas Muldowney, registered respiratory therapist/lung navigator

CHAPTER NINE

~~~~~~~~~~

YOU ARE NOT ALONE IN YOUR MANIFESTING JOURNEY

If You Can Trust in the Universe, You Can Trust Yourself

No matter how many people are around, life can feel lonely. Sometimes the more people that are around, the lonelier life feels. Although the feeling is valid, the universe has you and people in it—dead or alive, near or far—have you. If you can just trust the universe and know that is true, you can trust that you can do what you choose, that you have it within you to do that, whatever it is. We've got you. You've got this. It's time to fly.

I am a badass. I am not alone.

What makes me feel badass today?

I am a badass. I am not alone.

What fear will I face today?

I am a badass. I am not alone.

What can I do today to make me feel even
more badass?

I am a badass. I am not alone.

What fellow badass can I connect with today?

I am a badass. I am not alone.

Why is being a badass important to me?

I am a badass. I am not alone.

I don't like to play favorites, but I kind of want to
with this one. You are a badass and being a badass
means knowing you are supported. This can be
symbolic or literal support—that's up to you. The
universe can support you. Any person can support
you—dead or alive. Even someone you don't know
can serve as your support. Taylor, take the wheel!

For me, it's always been my grandfather, Papa
Herbie, both when he was alive and now that
he's moved on.

When I was eighteen years old, Papa Herbie died,
laying his head down on his desk and giving in to
the heart attack that even he couldn't say no to. He
was writing a letter—to me. He composed the letter,
signed his name, and died.

Papa Herbie was strong and handsome, and he
always wore a string tie and a hat with a feather in
it. He always had a pocket full of change that he
would rattle all day long. His shirts were cotton and
smelled like soap flakes.

The Ideal Diner had a different smell: a mix between
the sweet, syrupy smell of the pink disinfectant used
to clean the place and the hunger-inducing smell of
bacon frying in heavy, iron pans.

The diner was small, filled by only fourteen square
aluminum tables with Formica tops. Sometimes they
were wobbly, and Papa would rip off the cover of a
matchbook and fold it, tucking it under a table leg to
steady a table. Each table had four metal chairs with
shiny, plastic upholstered seats. Some of them were
held together by tape and luck alone.

Papa never let me sit in a ripped one.

Papa took me there every time he came to visit.
Early in the morning before my parents woke up,

Papa would be dressed and ready to go one hour before we were planning to head out.

He would drink a cup of boiling water at the dining room table. "Have to clean out the pipes," he'd say.

Then he'd lay out all his pills and swallow them down one by one. When I would ask why he had to take all of those oddly shaped tablets and multi-colored capsules, he would say, "I'm just gluing myself together. That's what you have to do when you get to be my age."

After he was done, he would wait in the car, his hands resting on the wheel. I think he just liked to be alone sometimes. When I'd go out to the carport to check on him, he'd be laying his head back onto the car's blue upholstered seat and he'd say, "I'm just resting my eggies." He always remembered to scrawl a note to my parents on the back of a discarded envelope so they would know where we had gone. "No need to waste a good piece of paper on our early morning antics," he'd say.

"You know where we are," he'd scrawl on the tattered flap of a faded envelope.

I always ordered the same thing: fried eggs, runny in the middle with the whites done through; two pieces of toast, no butter; and two strips of bacon. Papa would tell me stories about having to sleep over at Beacon Auto Parts when the storms were so bad that snow barred the doors. He'd spend the night in the ladies' room because it had a small fainting couch.

"I'd have to sleep with my legs dangling over the edge, but it was better than the garage floor. And there was a snack machine in there where I could get peanuts and chocolate bars for dinner," he'd say. "I'd look in everyone's desk for change." Then he'd laugh.

I'd laugh too. He always told the same stories, but I didn't mind.

"Her name was Betsey. She volunteered at the NSO giving out fruit punch in waxy paper cups. She was the most beautiful girl I'd ever seen, with shiny blond hair and blue eyes you could swim in," he'd say. "I could've married that girl." His voice would trail off, and he'd finish the rest of the story to himself in his head. Smiling, he'd savor the parts of the story that I now imagine were things a five-year-old had no business hearing.

Papa would let me pay the bill, counting crisp ones into my hand and reminding me to say, "Yes, ma'am" and "No, ma'am."

"Well, aren't you just the prettiest little thing," the woman at the register would say.

"Yes, ma'am," I'd respond. The woman would laugh and hand me the change. When I'd get back to the table with my hand out to give it to Papa, he'd refuse it. "Put that in your pocket,' he'd say, "and don't tell your parents. They don't understand us. We need our traveling money."

I'd grin and fill my pockets with the coins. I'd reach in and feel them all day long.

After we left the diner, we'd go straight to the toy store. I could pick anything out I wanted as long as it cost less than $5.00. Papa would write $5.00 down on a scrap of paper in large print so that I would know what numbers to look for on the boxes. For what seemed like hours spent in the toy store, I would ask, "Is $3.99 less than $5.00? Is $7.99 less than $5.00? Is $14.99 less than $5.00?"

Papa was so patient. He would answer me, smiling each time. He'd trail behind me along aisle after aisle until I made my choice.

"Oooooh," I'd finally gasp. "She's perfect." There was a beautiful baby doll that came with all the accessories: a crib, a high chair, a blanket, a bottle, diapers, and a change of clothes. "Is $19.99 less than $5.00?" I asked breathlessly. "It certainly is," Papa replied.

When we got to the car, he opened the door for me. It was magic riding in the car next to Papa. He hummed to the radio as I took my new doll out of the package, opening it carefully so as to not to lose any of her belongings or rip the box. Then I clutched the doll in one hand and laid the other on Papa's hand as it rested on the seat between us. I remember thinking that one day I would marry a man just like Papa.

"Look at this," I'd say rushing in the front door, thrusting my new treasures forward once we arrived back home. "Herbie, it's too much," my mom would say. "It was less than $5.00," I'd volunteer. My mother would look at Papa and shake her head. It would not be until I learned arithmetic that I knew why.

There were some mornings when we wouldn't make it to the diner or to the toy store. On those mornings, Papa seemed harried; usually that was after talking on the phone with Grandma about when he was returning home or about her son, Keith.

He would rest the receiver in the cradle and say, "I think I'm just gonna take the banana boat to Goona Goona." Or he'd say, "One of these days I'm gonna take the gas pipe." I didn't know what he meant, but it didn't sound good.

The Ideal Diner is gone now, and so is Papa. It was my father who called to tell me. "It's Daddy," I heard the voice on the other end of the receiver say. "Hi, Daddy," I said, "Happy Valentine's Day." "This isn't a happy call," he said. "What do you mean?" I asked.

"Papa's dead."

Apparently, I passed out. My roommate finished the call with my father, packed my things, and put me on a plane. The next thing I remember I was in Boston standing under the bus shelter in the rain waiting for the shuttle to take us to Auntie Caroline's.

I walked around the funeral in a daze. I couldn't talk to anyone, but I listened to them all.

"There's Jenny," someone would say, pointing to me and trying to whisper. "She was his favorite, you know. He went to all her plays and her rehearsals too. He wrote her love letters like the boys sent home from the war." Some would cluck their tongues in disapproval.

"Grandparents shouldn't play favorites," some of them would say. I knew my sister and cousins heard the talk too. I don't think anyone was surprised by it;

I wasn't. I didn't feel a bit bad about it either. Funny thing was none of them knew just how much he had "favored" me, giving me fifty-dollar bills every time he saw me.

"Don't tell your parents," he'd say, pressing the crisp bill into my hand and winking at me. I didn't know until after he died how little he could afford such gifts. I cried for months after that, and I still do, every Valentine's Day.

I filled the shovel with dirt at the cemetery as is the tradition and sprinkled it on his coffin as gently as I could. As we rode in the limousine, the cemetery fading from view in the back window, I swear I saw Papa standing on the street corner, rattling the change in his pockets.

Papa might not be here anymore in the traditional sense, but I know he is always here with me. I can feel and hear and see him. It's true. He replaces things I've lost. He cheers every win. He comforts me at every loss. And whenever I start to feel alone, I can sense him reminding me that that is simply not possible because he is always by my side.

Feeling lonely is a real thing, and it can happen even when you're in a crowd. When you feel unsupported; misunderstood; disconnected; disenfranchised; or when you feel like you can't be yourself, that can be very isolating. And when you feel isolated and alone, you feel anything but badass.

Having Papa is a comfort for which I am grateful beyond words. Everyone should be so lucky—to have that sense of acceptance, of being held—always. It's what you need in order to manifest what you desire. A badass is never truly alone.

You are not alone. Heck, I'm here, and I support all badasses. I support you. Take the leap. Accept the challenge. Enjoy the journey. You've got this, and we've got you. You're part of the circle of badasses. Trust the universe, it's got you. We've got you. Now's the time to trust yourself.

You are a badass.

You are not alone.

Let me hear you.

I am a badass.

I am not alone.

Yes!!

Manifesting Moments

"For me, the word 'manifesting' means 'to make real.' It means something was created and brought forth by some sort of consciousness, from the void of nothing into tangible reality. I've consciously and subconsciously manifested things in my life such as dream jobs, my career, relationships, adventures and scenarios. It's quite fun and a perk to what we call life!"

—Rey Medrano, celebrity makeup artist and psychic medium

"Manifesting to me is an essential part of life we aren't really taught about. I don't look at it as 'woo woo.' I think of it as setting an intention and putting that intention out into the world. By doing so, we take the actions to achieve that goal consciously and subconsciously. It's more about an alignment of energy for me."

—Dara Kaplan, partner & president at Wunderlich Kaplan Communications and founder of Dara Kaye Jewelry

"We are all able to dive into the mystical roads of manifestation. To me, you're either fully on the manifestation bus or you're under it. Doesn't it seem like the best choice is to always be *on* that bus? I recommend visualizing any time in the present or future to be filled with prosperity—from emotional to financial (and everything in between) as if it's already cascading into your bespoke Italian leather wallet.

Write affirmations like, 'My bank account is a symphony of zeros equaling many millions.' Surround yourself with all that you seek, including vision boards. The energy you put into anything will be returned tenfold. I have manifested plenty in my life, all my life—from travel to experiences, to yes, people. All of it shows up when we are energetically ready—really ready. So, what are you waiting for? Manifest everything you want starting *right now*. Remember, the universe loves a confident manifester like yourself. As pop psychology guru Dr. Wayne Dyer wrote, 'You'll see it when you believe it.' "

—Lance Avery Morgan, author; excerpted from his forthcoming book *Money Manners & Merit*

"When I lived in East Austin, I would regularly go to the Colorado River, relax in the water, and manifest peace, strength, and happiness. The water was cold and would wash over me while I manifested these wishes. I would close my eyes, breathe, and settle into my thoughts. I wouldn't get out of the water until I took a few long breaths and truly manifested these wishes. Shortly after, my wife and I started dating.

I basically manifest while I'm in nature. I always take time to breathe and sit in my thoughts, manifesting positivity, health, and so on. My wife even said, 'Why do you think I always come to you when I need to make something happen?' She used to call me the 'River Witch' because I'd always go to the river and manifest my thoughts."

—Lisa Hause, photographer

CHAPTER TEN

YOU CAN HANDLE WHATEVER COMES YOUR WAY

If You Can Handle the Worst, You'll Be Ready for the Best

There are many times in life when what you are facing feels impossible. If you're here reading these words, that means you got through that impossible situation. You did it. Somehow, some way, you did it. And if you did it before, you can do it again. The toughest part is believing you can. So, believe it. You've got this. And when you see all of the "impossible" things you can wrangle, just imagine how easy all the other things you need to do will be!

I am a badass.

I can do what feels impossible.

What makes me feel badass today?

I am a badass.

I can do what feels impossible.

What fear will I face today?

I am a badass.

I can do what feels impossible.

What can I do today to make me feel even more badass?

I am a badass.

I can do what feels impossible.

What fellow badass can I connect with today?

I am a badass.

I can do what feels impossible.

Why is being a badass important to me?

I am a badass.

I can do what feels impossible.

We have no idea what we are capable of until we are really put to the test. I know something for sure, though. You can do far more than you think you can. You can do what you might deem impossible.

I hope you never have to do the impossible. But it should be comforting to know you can. The thing is that for a badass, the impossible is just another bump in the road. You see, you are manifesting the most badass version of you, and she can handle things. She can handle everything.

That's why being a badass and badass manifesting the best version of you is so vital. Because you never know when the universe might just tap you on the shoulder and ask you to do the impossible...

"Your mother has cancer." Hearing the words through the telephone's receiver, I knew it was my father's voice.

I plopped onto my roommate's threadbare futon. The walls were covered in clown masks with hollow holes for eyes. "I want to talk to her," I told my father.

"I'm okay," my mother said.

"You're not. But you will be," I said. "I'm coming home."

I'm not sure where that came from. I hadn't thought about it before I said it. It was like my body just knew what had to be done even though my mind was telling me it was impossible. I was on tour with a children's theater company. I was a kid, just 25 years old. I didn't know how to take care of someone with cancer, especially my own mom.

But in that moment, something else took over, and before I knew it, I had put in my notice and driven to Baltimore.

It was hard to see her in bed like that, curled up on herself, dressed in faded sweats and wrapped in an old, wool blanket. She looked so small. Her room and her bed seemed bigger than I remembered.

I kept telling myself, "You can do this. You can do this. You can do this."

I remember the car ride to the hospital for her operation. My father and I both had our laptops. "See, this will be good," I remember my mother saying. "You can both finally get some work done."

At the hospital, they kept asking her a million questions. "Name. Address. Social Security Number. Date of Birth. Employer." I wanted to scream, "Shut up!" "My mother is dying!" "Leave her alone!" Then it got worse.

"In the instance of your untimely death during your hospital stay, do you wish to fill out a living will?" That was it. I saw the last bit of color drain from my mother's face and felt it all rise up in mine.

"No," I answered for her, "And you can get the rest of the information from my father. May I have my mother's room number please?"

She banded my mother's wrist. I held my mother's hand. "You'll be fine," I said to her. Neither of us believed me.

We went up to a tiny room where my mother was to change into a hospital gown. She looked like you could snap her bones between your fingers. I put all of her things in a bag. My father returned, then the doctor came in. It was time. I wanted to say "goodbye," "I love you," "thank you,"—something. You know, just in case. "You'll be fine," I said.

They wheeled my mother out into the hall. She was holding her hands in her lap and looking down at them. I didn't recognize her. I did recognize that posture, though; the way she cupped her hands and examined them as if for the first time. That's what she was doing.

That's how you knew. That something was wrong, I mean. Worry has always worn my mother. I gathered her things and left the room. I took the elevator to her "permanent" room. I remember wishing I could just click my heels three times.

It was at the end of the hall. The door was huge, the width of the room. I felt like Alice. It must have been used for a supply room or the like in its former life. With the door open, you could see the bed, facing you. It was like a lab where they do experiments.

I couldn't even go in. I went back to the front desk to have it changed.

"She can't be in that room. She won't get better."

I think she believed me. Or maybe it was just that I looked terrible. While her mouth explained that a switch was impossible, her fingers typed into the computer and then handed me a sticky with the number of my mother's new room. I don't remember leaving the desk or walking to the new room. I just remember being there.

I hung up my mother's things. I laid a pristine carton of crayons and a Winnie-the-Pooh coloring book on her bed tray.

Then we waited.

My father and I pretended to work. We pretended to eat lunch. We pretended to talk.

Finally, the doctor appeared. "She did very well. She'll be in her room shortly." It was strange, I didn't know how to react. I didn't want to seem too happy. I didn't want to provoke the "hospital gods." But we could be happy, right? "So, she's okay?" I asked.

"It's strictly a matter of wait and see: six months of radiation therapy, and we'll keep checking her. That's all we can do." She wasn't in the hospital long, just a day or two, until she could do things again, what few things anyone can do after major surgery.

Taking care of her was hard. We fought a lot. We had trouble finding things to talk about. I didn't like washing her or dressing her, and she didn't like me doing it. I kept wondering how we were making it work.

Because we both knew we had to, I figured. It was too hard for my dad. It was just too much. Though he was so used to taking care of other people and their families, this was way too close to home. This *was* home.

My mother slept a lot in the afternoon, and when she did, my father and I would have lunch at a

diner, grilled cheese sandwiches and tomato soup—
comfort food, like cinnamon toast.

He would take me to the candy store and buy me a
half pound of nonpareils. I love those little candies
with the smooth dark chocolate bottoms and the
bumpy white beads of sugar on top. I wondered
if it was okay to eat chocolate when your mother
has cancer.

My dad said it was. Even back then, before self-
care was the buzzword it is now, he knew that we
needed to take care of ourselves too if we were going
to take care of her. If we were to manifest our best
selves, we'd need a little help from the simplest of
pleasures, like simple meals and translucent bags
of candies.

My mother passed away in 2025. Her cancer never
returned. We never talk about those weeks when
I cared for her—never. But I think about it a lot. I
think about it because if you had asked me before
I spent time caring for her—even if you ask me
now—I would tell you it's impossible. I can't. It's too
hard. It's too scary. I don't like medical stuff. Surely
there's someone else.

But there wasn't. It was a job for a badass. And I
am a badass. I am up for the challenge, and I can
muster up the guts, the strength, the power, and

the magic to get things done even when things are going through my mind, saying things like you're too young, and no daughter in her early twenties should ever have to care for her mother. She shouldn't have to. But if she has to, she should. My mother and I have had a tough go of it when it comes to our relationship. But she needed me. And I knew myself then like I know myself now. The more impossible the task, the more I need to prove to myself that I can tackle it.

And this applies not just to emotionally impossible things or medical or health-related issues that seem impossible. It also applies to anything that you feel you're not smart enough or strong enough or talented enough or resourceful enough or whatever enough to accomplish. Sure, there are some limitations. No amount of manifesting is going to get me on the Detroit Lions...as a player.

But I could certainly become the team nutritionist, the public relations director, or heck, the owner! If the goal is to be part of the team, the goal is only impossible if I set truly impossible expectations like my becoming big enough and strong enough to play pro football. Otherwise, the sky's the limit.

Okay, if something is truly impossible by definition, fine. But we are talking about *seemingly* impossible things here, and those obstacles can be overcome

if you believe they can and you do the work to
make it so.

The mantra is that you can do what feels impossible.
But *how you feel* can change. So, change it. Instead
of "It's impossible for me to be on the Detroit
Lions," I can say, "It's impossible for me to *play*
on the Detroit Lions. But I will be a member of the
team one day!"

Being a badass is knowing you can. Badass
manifesting is doing what has to be done to make
it happen.

I don't wish the impossible on anyone. But it will
happen to most of us in one way or another at one
time or another. So, slip into your invisible badass
armor and manifest your best self. You can do this.
You can do anything. You get to decide. And I can't
imagine you'd decide that any old thing is going to
take you down.

Manifest a life that stands up to the impossible.

You are a badass.

You can do what feels impossible.

This is true. So, say it out loud like it's true.

I am a badass.

I can do what feels impossible.

You most certainly can!!

Manifesting Moments

"Manifesting and manifestation as concepts make
me think more from a metaphysical viewpoint. Not
that I really think it's evoking magic, but I do think
it's more heavily related to our intuition and how in
tune we are with the universe. To me, manifestation
is more about being in harmony with the universe
and its flow. When I'm aligned with my true self,
I just sort of seem to end up where I need to be
and in front of who I need to be in front of. I don't
necessarily think I manifested Virginia—I was so
dead set against getting married that I'm pretty sure
she manifested me.

But there have been people I've felt I was meant
to know in some capacity when I've met them and
who have handed me little tokens of wisdom that
kept me moving. Meeting Cher's best friend when
I was twenty-one and having her to talk to for a
while, ending up in music journalism, meeting Mary
Chapin and having her hold my hands and tell me
to basically let the fuck go: All of those very small
encounters led up to the big things for me.

PS: I'm a natural born pessimist and have manifested
things with no optimism in sight. That's why for me,

it doesn't feel so much like a mindset but an innate ability to align."

—Alyssa Moore, writer

"Yesterday my friend prayed with me, and she said, 'Let us stay humble but not have life humble us.' She focused on that because I had written my workout goal was to be humbled and not push myself too hard. During my morning meditation, I kept thinking about that. I have been manifesting the wrong thing, because life has been humbling the shit out of me recently, and I always say, 'It's good when life humbles us.' Um…that means I've been asking the universe to kick my ass over and over. So I'm on a new mental track today and back to feeling more positive, and I will *never* use the word humble in the wrong way again.

The point is that how we manifest is so important. We should refer to whatever it is we are trying to manifest in the present, as if we are already embodying whatever we are manifesting, or that we already have whatever it is. The word manifest evokes the word 'necessary' for me. We should set an intention for our day or manifest our ideal day *every day*."

—Heather Nixon, yoga and breathwork instructor

CHAPTER ELEVEN

YOU CAN OPEN YOURSELF TO OTHERS AND EXPAND YOUR MANIFESTING POWERS

If You Can Let Others In, You Can Find Your Way in the World

Making things happen can feel isolating. Sometimes, that isolation even seems necessary. We don't want anyone to steal our energy or our joy—or our ideas for that matter! But the truth is, being around your herd will make you more able to achieve your dreams. Being surrounded by other badasses can feel empowering. You can look around and know that all of those other people are making their dreams come true. And if they can do it, you can too!

I am a badass.

It's badass to be around other badasses.

What makes me feel badass today?

I am a badass.

It's badass to be around other badasses.

What fear will I face today?

I am a badass.

It's badass to be around other badasses.

What can I do today to make me feel even more badass?

I am a badass.

It's badass to be around other badasses.

What fellow badass can I connect with today?

I am a badass.

It's badass to be around other badasses.

Why is being a badass important to me?

I am a badass.

It's badass to be around other badasses.

I'm not sure why this was such a tough nut for me to crack at first. I used to think I needed to be the only badass in the room, or the best one, or the biggest one to somehow prove I *was* one. But no more. Now, I surround myself with badasses. Being surrounded by badasses doesn't make me less of a badass. It makes me more of one.

Being a badass has nothing to do with comparing yourself to anyone else. Everyone gets to be their own badass self, whatever that looks like. It certainly looks different for everyone. But isn't that kind of the best part of badassery?

Who cares what anyone else thinks. Be where you feel like a rock star because you are a rock star. Comic-Con? Yes! Quilt conference? Yes! Prom themed purse bingo? Absolutely!

My friend Justine told me once that it's important to have three kinds of friends—ones who are just like you, ones who you aspire to be like, and ones to whom you can be a mentor. I love that.

And here's the thing. All three types can be badasses like you—just different kinds!

So, how do you go about finding your badass herd? Well, you start by seeking out activities and places and groups where you can imagine finding like-minded people. For many years, I went to a writers' and artists' commune outside of Charlottesville,

Virginia, called Nimrod, where I was able to add all three of those kinds of friends to my herd.

Every summer for up to a month, we would work, play, eat, and laugh together. At one point, I believe our ages ranged from twenty-five to eighty-five. So don't ever let age be a barrier. Writing is what brought us together. Our humanity is what kept us together. (More on that shortly...)

Now, this can go terribly wrong. There is a villain in the creation of herds, and its name is Envy.

I went to the famed Bread Loaf writers' retreat. I was so excited. I didn't learn until after attending that there is a self-imposed hierarchy between the writers that doesn't have to do with talent or success. It had to do only with how you were there. If you were there on a grant, you were a rock star. If you paid to attend, you were a peon.

I paid.

I let that make me feel small. Perhaps it was set up to make me feel that way, but I allowed it to make me feel small despite the fact that I was the only writer at the retreat other than the instructors who had already published a book and was working on the next. I even booked an appearance on the *Tyra*

Banks Show while there and still managed to let myself feel small.

My advice? Avoid those situations at all costs. Avoid places, people, and events that don't care who you are, or those focused on one-upmanship. I refuse to participate in that any longer. I love some healthy competition, but that's about respecting one another and raising one another up. Anything that's about tearing other people down, you can count me out. And I recommend you do the same. You don't need them, and they don't deserve you.

Surrounding yourself with badasses will make you feel like more of a badass. I feel the most badass at workshops and festivals—places where you are surrounded by like-minded people. I learned that magic trick in high school, a place where there were all sorts of badasses around me. But I was so extremely concerned with fitting in with the "cool kids" that I had a tough time finding my own way.

I became very self-conscious the summer before I entered high school. Everything about me suddenly seemed wrong—my hair, my nose, my clothes, my body, my interests—it all just seemed backwards and babyish and not okay. And camp that summer cemented my feelings. I was a student at the John Carroll School, a private, Catholic school that I had begged my parents to allow me to attend.

It seemed like all the girls were blonde and had boobs already: They looked like women. They wore makeup and knew how to flirt with boys. I was a geek and felt like one. I cut my hair into an asymmetrical bob, put safety pins in my ears, and joined the drama club.

I was lucky in some ways, I guess. Although I never got invited to the weekend field parties or was asked to any school dances (except by boys on the debate team or in the drama or Latin clubs), I could sit anywhere I liked in the cafeteria. This was no small feat in high school. One of my best friends was head cheerleader.

Don't ask me how that worked. I suppose I was good enough to hang out with at school—in moderation, of course—but anything more than that, like any invitation to sneak out for lunch or go to a party on the weekend, was just out of the question. The funny thing was I led sort of a double life. Although school was of course my primary pursuit, I also went away several times a year on what we called conclaves.

Conclaves were youth group events sponsored by synagogues throughout the region. Now, we certainly did attend services, take part in workshops, and learn Israeli folk dancing. But I have to be honest with you here. Conclaves were basically where I first dabbled in sex, drugs, and alcohol.

You see for some reason, I guess because these were supposed to be religious events, the girls and guys were allowed to stay together. We would sometimes sleep over at the hosting synagogue, but more often, we would stay with different "host families"—with six to ten teenagers per house depending on its size. We'd all be allowed to stay together in the oversized family room or finished basement.

The contradiction for me was that I was very popular at MAFTY (Mid-Atlantic Federation of Temple Youth) events. Now, I know what you're thinking. Sure, I was popular—I was queen of the geeks. But these kids weren't geeks, they were attractive—even by my snobby school's standards. They were smart and funny, as well as affluent. I had a million friends and plenty of male attention.

It was actually incredibly confusing. I remember crying uncontrollably every time I left one of the weekend-long events. I even remember praying (they were religious retreats, after all) that God would turn back the clock just this once, I'd do anything, *anything* to be able to live out the weekend all over again. It never worked, of course, but you can't blame a girl for trying.

I was a badass among badasses there, and I knew that was something I would seek out from then on. And I have been lucky enough to find it time and time again at places like the writers' weekends at the aforementioned Nimrod Hall before it sadly changed hands.

Nimrod was a long-held family property that hosted families, artists, and writers year after year. It was like Badass Heaven. For anywhere from one to eight weeks every summer, you could live in the mountains of Southwest Virginia and enjoy three home-cooked meals a day while spending your time taking long walks, tubing down the river, or simply rocking on the porch, sipping whiskey from a red Solo Cup as hummingbirds whizzed between brightly colored feeders.

If you were there as an artist or writer, you had what felt like endless hours to write or paint among your peers. In our writing group, ages ranged from people in their twenties to eighties. Skill levels varied from beginner to award-winning author. But support was at 100 percent for everyone all the time. Writing critiques included as many compliments as suggestions for improvement. Nimrod made me a writer. But perhaps more importantly, it lifted me up as a badass. Nimrod was a haven for badass writer women.

I never felt envious there even though there was plenty of reason to be if you chose that route. Instead, I felt the desire to celebrate the successes of the women around me because I knew that their successes didn't take away from mine. And being surrounded by success just seems to beget more success for yourself and those around you. I loved it.

Fern Fest was like that for me too. It's a women's music festival that takes place every summer in Michigan. It too makes me feel big and strong and small and squishy and funny and kind and generous—basically I feel like my true self. There, I emceed for the musicians' performances, I host a workshop on beading bracelets, and I swim in the support and love and talent that surrounds me in that context.

I am a summer camp girl, I always say: Camp Nottingham, Girl Scout Camp, Camp Louise (except that one summer), MAFTY, KUTZ, Lightning in a Bottle, Fern Fest, Feast Portland (which is sadly no more), Big Mouth Girl and even conferences, workshops, and trainings. I thrive in a herd of my people. You can too, so seek them out.

It's amazing to be in a totally immersive situation. But meet-ups and clubs can give you a similar fix: book clubs, crochet club, pickle ball club, wine club, bunko, mahjong, you get the idea. Find your badasses and circle up.

Once you experience being with your people, lifting others up, and feeling the joy of being able to be yourself, you will feel the kind of boost that you can't get anywhere else. You will feel more confident and more motivated. You will have more trust in who you are, what you want, and what you can do.

Don't shy away from connections. Don't do the "She'll steal my thunder" thing. Revel in similarities you discover you share with others and find your place and your power among your fellow badasses. You don't have to be an island. That shit is hard. All you have to be is you, and there are so many people who are ready to watch you shine.

You are a badass.

It's badass to be around other badasses.

Loud enough for the cheap seats to hear:

I am a badass.

It's badass to be around other badasses.

It sure as heck is!

Manifesting Moments

"To me, manifesting means setting a focused intention and believing wholeheartedly in the vision of what you want to bring into your life. It's not just about wishing; it's a combination of clear intention, belief, and action toward creating that reality.

I have definitely manifested things in my life. One example is my journey with B. Stuyvesant Champagne. It began as a dream, one fueled by my love and passion for champagne. I envisioned creating a brand that not only celebrated champagne but also represented my heritage and entrepreneurial spirit. Through persistent work, believing in that vision, and taking every opportunity to make it real, it has come to life. Manifesting, for me, has always been about aligning belief with action."

—Marvina Robinson, founder and CEO, B. Stuyvesant™ Champagne

"Okay, so true story: before manifesting became the term that we all know today, I used to think that I had premonitions—for real.

That's because when I wanted something or had a vision of how I wanted a room to look while decorating, I would envision it in my mind and direct all my energy into making it happen. What I didn't realize at the time was that I was actually manifesting my vision. So when I 'see' something the way I want it or 'see' something as if it is in my possession, I feel like I put that energy out into the universe and will it to come to me—and it usually does! Maybe not quickly, but eventually—when it's meant to be—it happens, and my vision comes to fruition."

—Danny Villareal, interior decorator

"To me, manifestation is the energy you give off to the universe in your efforts to steer your life in a desired direction. Manifesting alone isn't enough, it has to be done in conjunction with action that will lead you to where you want to be. I think manifesting has gotten a bad rap due to social media and so many people preaching about the topic. I think it's simply a different way to approach your goals in a way that will help your life move forward with abundance. I also believe that that you can manifest things in a negative way. If you put out negative energy into the universe, this is what will realize itself in your life. I think we have to be cautious about what we speak out into existence. I try my best to manifest positive things in my life like good health, healthy finances, and lots of love from friends and family.

I am not an avid manifester, but earlier this year, when I found an opening for a job that I loved, I tried to manifest it into existence for myself by speaking it out loud into the universe. I would say out loud that this position was 'mine,' and I would talk to my friends and loved ones about how I was ready for this role. I think that speaking in this way and putting it out into the universe gave me the confidence to present my best self throughout the interview process.

'Manifesting' this new job even helped me to believe that I was worthy of this job and that making this move would be a positive change in my life. Along with manifesting, I took action by taking steps to prepare for interviews and learn more about the company. In the end, I got the job, and in some ways, I feel as if the manifesting I did throughout the interview process really helped with the end result."

—Luis Morales, visual merchandising manager, Louis Vuitton

CHAPTER TWELVE

~~~~~~~~~~~~~~~

YOU CAN TAKE A CHANCE ON YOURSELF AND TRUST YOUR CHOICES

If You Can Take a Chance on Yourself, You'll Give Yourself More than Just a Chance

It's easy to follow the band. It's easy to go where everyone else is going. It's easy to keep doing what you've always done. But the same recipe yields the same meal. The same path leads to the same destination. The same decisions lead to the same results. If you want something new, do something new. Try the thing you haven't tried and you just might get what you haven't gotten.

I am a badass.

I am always open to the road less traveled.

What makes me feel badass today?

I am a badass.

I am always open to the road less traveled.

What fear will I face today?

I am a badass.

I am always open to the road less traveled.

What can I do today to make me feel even more badass?

I am a badass.

I am always open to the road less traveled.

What fellow badass can I connect with today?

I am a badass.

I am always open to the road less traveled.

Why is being a badass important to me?

I am a badass.

I am always open to the road less traveled.

I spent a lot of time scared. I spent a lot of time accepting what seemed to be the "right" path. I turned down a theater scholarship because I would never get a "real job" if I stayed with theater. I majored in English because "that's what I was good at." I went to law school because "that's what

English majors do." All along the way, I ignored the signs and options and possibilities.

What I wanted was to be an actress, to perform, to make my mark. What I was doing was what I was told and not what I desired. I wanted to go to NYU. I wanted to go to Boston College. I wanted to spread my wings. But when my mom said no to both, I simply accepted that. It's a regret I try hard not to have. But it lingers. I tried to follow the path that was basically laid out for me.

I was lucky, right? I was smart. My parents were paying for school. I needed to get out of dreamland and into the real world ahead. But in 1993, at twenty-three years old, I couldn't seem to do it anymore. I had to try the road less traveled because the road I was on was smothering me.

I decided to drop out of law school and join the closest thing to the circus I could manage: a touring children's theater company. Besides, I wasn't very good at law school despite everyone saying I was perfect for it.

So, on winter break of my second year, I called my father and told him I didn't want to go to law school anymore.

"So, why go back?" he'd said to me over the phone. "If you hate it—if you can't do it—don't go back." I was stunned. "But what will I do?" I asked.

"What do you mean? You always think of something else to do. You always make it work. That's what you're so good at." My father is amazing. It's unfortunate that he hadn't been able to override my mother during all those years of saying "no." She was always so scared for me, so unnecessarily and overwhelmingly scared. And fear can be dangerous and contagious.

But I took his advice, faxed in my "resignation," and answered an ad for a children's theater tour.

I had gone to the audition thinking, "If they hire me, I will go." Hire me they did, and so off I went in a dilapidated gray van tightly packed with costumes, sets, props, and the five of us.

First, we traveled mainly throughout central Virginia. Then we crisscrossed the southeastern states: Mississippi, North Carolina, South Carolina, West Virginia. Finally, we crept a bit northeast into Maryland, Delaware, and Pennsylvania.

We stayed in hotels that were only as safe and clean as the theater company manager deemed necessary to keep us from suing.

We spent weeks at a time on the road, covering mile after mile in that gray, seven-seat passenger van with no exterior markings save for scratches, scrapes, and dents. Many a neighborhood busybody called our van in, suspecting "illicit activity." But there were no drugs nor teenage runaways inside, just five people, ten costumes, one set, three puppets, and a multitude of props whose identities would reveal little to nothing about the drama that we twice daily performed. We looked like vagabonds with an odd proclivity for stealing the bizarre.

All along the way was dirt I didn't recognize: the crags of the West Virginia mountainsides, the red clay of the Tennessee hills, and the rich mud of the North Carolina farms and fields. Never were two nights spent in the same state, and never did we come to know more about a place than where to find the local Morrison's and nearest Walmart.

We knew each other so well after driving hundreds of miles together that there were times with little left to say. We fought, we laughed, and we dashed from state to state, escaping like thieves from each location, leaving nothing behind but shadows and smiles.

In fact, we rode constant swells of exhilaration from the curtain's twice daily rising and suffered equally predictable waves of exhaustion that blanketed us after the curtain fell. Setting up and tearing down, performing, greeting, driving, checking in, checking out. It was a blur of Comfort Inns and Chinese restaurants with names like Yum Yum and Chen's Den nestled in roadside strip malls.

We had to be it all since it was such a small tour: actor, props mistress, costume master, set designer, sound engineer, van maintenance roadie, travel agent, navigator. That last one demanded skills which none of us seemed to possess, and we found ourselves getting lost on a daily basis.

It was a wild existence. I spent each morning battling imagined monsters, climbing a foam beanstalk, and talking to a golden goose puppet. And I spent every night looking for the best of the worst on another sticky, plastic menu, grateful for the van full of weirdos with whom I was lucky enough to share this adventure.

When the tour ended and we turned in our costumes, we headed back to our respective homes to assimilate once again into our previous lives. I was grateful for four walls and a safe, warm, and familiar bed to sleep in every night. But even so, at least every now and again, I miss hearing the magic harp sing. Law school, though? There's not a single thing I miss about that. And the reason why is simple. It wasn't me. It was never me. It was the imagined me imagined by everyone but me.

The thing is, I never would have known if I hadn't taken those trips, both the one to law school and the one in the van.

Then there was the trip to Springfield, Illinois, where I lived for a season as part of a summer stock theater company—The Great American People Show.

We lived in a "condemned" building rumored to have once been an asylum for the mentally ill. I don't know if it really was condemned or if it ever had been an asylum. But I do know that I had an amazing time that summer, just as I did the summer after as a dancer at The Lost Colony in Manteo, North Carolina. That, too, was a magical experience, all thanks to taking the road less traveled.

On paper, they were crazy ideas. I didn't know anyone who had done those things before. There was no tutorial, no Google, way to do a deep dive, other than to literally dive in. I never would have known what a badass I am, or how capable I am of manifesting a badass life, if I hadn't tried.

I made the calls.

I found the opportunities.

I went to the auditions.

I went to the callbacks.

I said yes.

I wanted it. I could see it in my mind's eye, and then I captured it. It wasn't even necessarily that clear of a vision. I just knew I wanted to travel and act—so I did. Could I have moved to New York or LA? Sure. Could I have gotten an agent? Yup. Gone to acting school? Totally. Why didn't I? I don't know. Maybe I was afraid to fail. Maybe I didn't want what I thought I wanted. All I know is the things that happen for me happen because I want them and I take the steps.

You have to want it.

And you *have* to take the steps.

When I was finished with the tours and the summer stock theater, I called the university where I'd done my undergrad degree, Virginia Commonwealth.

"Hi! It's Jenny Block," I said into the receiver. "I want to come back. I want to give grad school a shot." A favorite receptionist in the small department answered, and I could hear as she put her hand over the mouthpiece and yelled out, presumably to the department chair, "It's Jenny Block. She wants to come back." I couldn't hear the reply. But then the receptionist got back on the phone.

"Dr. Fine says, 'Sounds good!' He'll get you set up with an application, and there's one teaching fellowship open. He said it's all yours if you want it!" I think I screamed right into the phone. "Yes! Thank you! Yes!" I cheered. "I figured that's what that hollering meant. See you next week!" she said.

I went back to graduate school. I taught for more than ten years. And then I began writing and speaking, and here I am five books and innumerable articles, speaking engagements, stand-up shows, and emcee gigs later! It's a road I never planned to take. I followed its curves, I made the efforts, and I continue to make them every day, because every day I get a little closer to that imaginary, "I made it!" that lives in my head.

Sometimes, the place you want to be is somewhere you don't even know about yet. I sure didn't know this is where I would land! That is why being open to the road less traveled is the best way to be. Don't block what the universe has in store for you. Find the path that makes it easier for it to find you...

You are a badass.

You are always open to the road less traveled.

Deep breath. Say it with intention.

I am a badass.

I am always open to the road less traveled.

You are, my friend. You really, really are.

Manifesting Moments

"To me, manifesting means to open your mind and your heart so that beautiful things can be brought into being. It means calling on your higher self to combine forces with the universe, allowing your life to be filled with the abundance you surely deserve. Manifesting is requesting access to the infinite power that you possess as a being in this solar system, and only when requested in complete humility can this power be obtained."

—Jessie Jensen, Certified Doula (DTI)

"Manifesting to me means visualizing an outcome and then achieving it. I have manifested my upcoming TV show by saying, 'I want to write and star in my own comedy TV show' for years until it finally happened."

—Tim Murray, comedian, writer, and actor

"In 2016, I meditated on the words Patience and Faith around finding my romantic partner and my first big Broadway job. I wrote down the goals every day, visualized them, saw them, felt them, made space in my life for them, and by December, Tim and I had gone on our first date and I booked the Aladdin and my first national tour. It really does work!"

—Michael Bullard, actor

"I was literally just talking about this to one of my team members this week as she asked me how I got my job, and I told her I always get what I want. It just doesn't always come when you want it or how you want it, but I truly believe whatever you want to happen will happen if you show it's meant to be.

In my mind, manifesting starts with knowing what you want or want to achieve. It's not as easy as it sounds. One of the greatest things about really wanting something and truly believing it will happen is it forces you to focus on what it is you want. I truly believe I manifested my husband and my current role at work."

—Julie Estrada, public relations director, North America, Merlin Entertainments

"I believe the term 'manifest' is one of the terms most overused by some people who have dreams but don't put any action into creating a plan that 'manifests' what they desire into a reality for themselves. A lot of people spend more time planning their vacation then they do in planning the manifestation of their success."

—Hayden Walker, writer and founder, *Austin Food Magazine*

CHAPTER THIRTEEN

YOU CAN SAY NO WITHOUT FEELING GUILTY TO PROTECT YOUR BADASSERY

If You Sometimes Say No to Others, You Can Always Say Yes to Yourself

It's hard; I get it. As a people pleaser myself, I hate to say no. Even when I'm too busy, even when I don't want to do the thing, even when I know I'm not going to get my own stuff done, I say yes. But when I say yes when I shouldn't, I am saying no to myself. Manifesting my badass life means saying yes to my badass self, which means sometimes saying no to others. Be kind; be direct; be respectful. But be true to yourself.

I am a badass.

A badass always says yes (even when they're saying no).

What makes me feel badass today?

I am a badass.

A badass always says yes (even when they're saying no).

What fear will I face today?

I am a badass.

A badass always says yes (even when they're saying no).

What can I do today to make me feel even more badass?

I am a badass.

A badass always says yes (even when they're saying no).

What fellow badass can I connect with today?

I am a badass.

A badass always says yes (even when they're saying no).

Why is being a badass important to me?

I am a badass.

A badass always says yes (even when they're saying no).

Sometimes when you say no to someone else, it's because you are saying yes to yourself. That can be a tough thing to do. I have grown very accustomed to saying yes despite my own needs, desires, and bandwidth. Every day I work hard to think before I just say yes.

What I try to keep in mind is that when I say no to something, it's because I'm saying yes to myself—to my sanity, to my peace, and to my passions. I am saying yes to me. And that's a good thing. I not only have a right to take care of myself, I also have a responsibility to do so.

The truth is that the only way I can bring my whole badass self to each day and each task is by taking care of myself. The only way I can manifest the badass life of my dreams is to take care of myself. If I burn myself out, I'm done. Then, I won't be able to help anyone, myself included.

One thing that has really helped me on my "learning to say no to others in order to say yes to me" journey is something that my writing mentor, Charlotte Morgan, taught me many years ago. Charlotte always said that instead of saying no when someone asks you to do something that you either don't want to do, can't do, or won't do, respond with, "It's simply not possible."

She told me, "It's much harder to argue with, 'It's simply not possible.' "

"Why?"

"It's simply not possible."

"But why?"

"Because it's simply *not* possible." As simple as that. You have permission to say no—always.

I have often wondered why it is so hard to say no. And I think the answer is painfully obvious; it's because most of us, and women in particular, don't want to upset anyone, disappoint anyone, "make" anyone "feel bad," create more work for someone else, or let someone down.

You get the idea.

All too many of us are people pleasers, and we will do nearly anything to please others without thinking about how we are hurting ourselves. Here's the thing: Although we may be saying yes in the moment to please others, we are ultimately doing a disservice to everyone involved. Why? Because we are hiding our badass light under a bushel. I'll explain.

When we say yes to things we want—or need—to say no to, we become resentful, whether we realize it or not. And when we walk through the world from resentfulness tucked inside of us, we are not acting from kindness, abundance, or joy, we are acting with pain. And pain begets more pain. Saying yes when we should say no leads to stress. It leads to feeling overburdened, put upon, angry with those who put us in that position, and angry with ourselves for allowing it.

Just recently, I was at an amazing event where they sprang an after-hours scavenger hunt on us. It had already been a long—albeit wonderful—day. But it was time to eat dinner and unwind, and instead, I was asked to walk and Uber all around town taking selfies with my teammates.

I was so torn. I want to be fun; I want to participate; I want to be seen as a "good egg." However, I also was not a huge fan of my team lead's bossiness and lack of planning. I hadn't slept the night before, and I had a big weekend of training ahead. So I knew what the result would be if I went along for the ride.

At first, I tried to play along. But after one stop, I knew it was just not a good idea for me. I fibbed a bit and said I had work due. I did have work—but it could have waited. I felt relieved but also guilty. I told my daughter, and you know what her twenty-five-year-old self said to me? "Good job advocating for yourself!" I didn't know whether to giggle or beam with pride—or both.

She was right, of course. That was exactly what I had done and precisely what I needed to do. And of course, my teammates understood. I'm an adult. I was doing what I needed to do.

Now I want to be honest here—as I believe you always should be with your doctor, your bartender, and your readers: I did stew over this for a bit. What did my teammates really think? What would the people running the event think? What if everyone was talking about how terrible I was? What if I never got invited back? I was spinning like a top.

But then, my friend Justine said, "Ball it up and toss it out the window. That's not yours."

"That's not yours," I said over again in my head.

I don't think I'll ever forget those words as long as I live. So much of what plagues so many of us, keeps us from living our best lives, and stops us from doing the badass manifesting that we deserve is worrying about stuff that's not even ours.

What other people think of us is not our problem.

Think about that for a minute. If you could cut out of your brain everything that doesn't really belong to you, that is not really your problem, how much extra room would you have for making things happen?

That's the secret sauce. A badass knows what's hers and what isn't and doesn't waste time or energy on other people' stuff. We have to say no to what's not meant for us. And when we say no to all of that extra nonsense, we are ultimately saying yes to ourselves and the lives of our dreams.

Once again, I hearkened back to those words my dad had said when I got that first piece of hate mail. "Jenny, I mean this in the nicest possible way. But no one cares about you," he said. I was offended at first, but then I let it sink in. He didn't mean that no one loves me or no one cares *about* me. He meant that deep down, no one is worried about whether or not I go on the scavenger hunt, or what I write about that concert I saw, or whether I have on pink socks or white ones.

Most of us are far too busy with our own lives to worry about much else. I mean, do you care if a friend said no to an event or doesn't share your love for *Fraggle Rock* or hates socks altogether? Maybe it matters when it comes to who your closest friends are or who you marry. But perhaps it matters even less then. The fact of the matter is, most of what we are holding ourselves back from because of other people and what they might think is bonkers, because—no one cares.

It's good that you want to help everyone. It's nice that you want to say yes to everything. It comes from a good place, I get that. But if it's hurting you, it's not actually a good thing. And anyone who loves you would not want you to say yes to things that are hurting you.

It's okay to tell the truth. And it's also okay to just say, "It's simply not possible." You don't owe your soul to anyone. And sometimes people will be disappointed because they are so incredibly used to you saying yes, and that's okay too. That's their problem, not yours. This is about your badass life, which you wholly deserve. No one has the right to suck the life force out of you and make it impossible to manifest what is rightfully yours.

The kids can go without going to the park this one time. Your partner can eat a frozen pizza. Someone else can bake for that party. The school or the church or whatever other group can call someone else. There are lots of people who never say yes—now's their time. This isn't a group project in high school. You don't have to do it all yourself.

I promise, you will still get an A in my book for self-care and badass manifesting!

On an airplane, they always tell you to put on your own oxygen mask before helping anyone else. That's because you're of no use to anyone, including yourself, if you pass out. And then, someone will have to attend to you as well as the people you could have helped. Saying no to things that are not for you is just like putting on your oxygen mask first.

There is no other way for you to truly manifest your badass self and your badass life.

So say no. Say no when you can't or won't or simply don't want to say yes. When you're out of bandwidth, you're out of bandwidth. And when you say yes to too much, you can't do anything well. So, saying yes to everything is actually a disservice to all the things. Life is short. Say yes to what is meant for you and no to the rest.

A badass knows she can say no.

A badass always says yes—to herself—which sometimes means saying no.

You're a badass.

A badass always says yes to life (even when they're saying no).

Look right into the mirror and into your own eyes and speak truth into reality.

I am a badass.

A badass always says yes to life (even when they're saying no).

Speak up! Speak now!

Manifesting Moments

"To me, manifesting is casting a spell. It's telling the universe, but also your own body, what it is that you want, or what you feel the world needs. Have I ever manifested something? Yes. Somehow even in patriarchy, I have manifested a feminist dream of making my own empowered, radical, feminist art in the midst of a patriarchal nightmare. So in a way, it's like manifesting is having the courage to name something and then either speak it or envision it as something, so it starts to vibrate outside of you."

—Bitch, musician and performance artist

"Manifestation is to me the embodiment of the natural laws of the universe. It is harnessing the law of attraction within our cells, our spirits, and minds. As we align our intentions with our way of being, like attracts like.

The power of manifestation works in both directions, positive and negative. But through my own life experience and the knowledge base shared by spiritual warriors and physicists, I have found the negative is thousands of times weaker than the positive.

Luck is a matter of preparation meeting opportunity. Intentions tell the universe where to put the opportunities we desire. They are dropped in the path we have set before ourselves. If we stray from our intentional path, we miss the opps.

Recently I heard someone speaking of being very careful about setting intentions. They are in direct relationship to manifesting and our integrity to ourselves. If I like to be lazy, it's best to be very careful about not setting unattainable goals. Trusting ourselves and standing in a way true to our own integrity is the key to unlocking the power of manifestation."

—Tiffany Christopher, singer/songwriter

CHAPTER FOURTEEN

YOU CAN HANDLE COMPLIMENTS AND COMPLAINTS WITH EASE

If You Can Absorb the Love, You Can Deflect the Hate

It's a strange thing. One person says one mean thing, and it sticks like tar. But a million kind words? Most people can't take those in. That has to change. If someone has something unkind to say, that's about them, not you. Let that slide off into the nothingness. And when someone says something lovely, capture that, repeat it in your head, and save it for a rainy day. Those kind words are all about you, and you deserve to revel in them.

I am a badass.

I can take a compliment, and I can reply to my own complaint box.

What makes me feel badass today?

I am a badass. I can take a compliment, and I can reply to my own complaint box.

What fear will I face today?

I am a badass. I can take a compliment, and I can reply to my own complaint box.

What can I do today to make me feel even more badass?

I am a badass. I can take a compliment, and I can reply to my own complaint box.

What fellow badass can I connect with today?

I am a badass. I can take a compliment, and I can reply to my own complaint box.

Why is being a badass important to me?

I am a badass. I can take a compliment, and I can reply to my own complaint box.

Badasses don't need other people to compliment them. But it doesn't hurt if they do. And just because we don't need compliments doesn't mean we can't or don't want them. Let's not kid ourselves, it feels good to have someone recognize our accomplishments and our hard work.

I honestly wish people gave stickers to adults the way we do for kids: "Way to go!" on a lightning bolt; "Right on!" written on a balled fist; "You're a star!" on a bright yellow star; "You're the grapest!" on a scratch-and-sniff bunch of grapes; "You rocked this!" on a guitar.

But alas, it's unlikely that will happen. Instead, you can create a compliment box. Write down the things people say to you and cut and paste the ones emailed or texted to you. Circle back when you need a little boost.

Mine includes notes from wedding couples. I have written about in the New York Times. Here are a few of my favorites:

From bride, Kathryn "Kiwi" Mullen:

> I have literally sent this to all my friends and read it a million times over. Wes surprised me and framed the article *just* this morning!!!! This is the happiest day ever. Genuinely cannot express my gratitude to you. Next time you're cooped up in the little study of yours at home, you better *remember* how impactful your work is and how honored people are to be featured by you.

And she wrote me again.

Just wanted to reach out and say thank you
again. I'm sure I sound like a broken record,
but it's been *so* fun to have people all over
the country send me screenshots of them
coming across it; coworkers who I hardly
know, friends I haven't talked to in ages,
family on both sides... Ah! I feel famous! Did
I pay $199 to have a plaque of it? *Yes!* Do
I regret it? No! You wrote it so beautifully,
and we are still so honored to have it
out there.

From Mitra Ghahramani, a source for an article for
the *New York Times* on the Sofreh Aghd:

You are an amazing author, by the way. Love
the way you wrote everything so beautifully
that even with me knowing all the details,
reading your articles made me fall in love
with the *sofreh* and our culture again.

From the mother of one of my *New York Times*
brides, Heather Lynn Certner Brugger, the artist
behind Heather Lynn Arts:

Jenny, you outdid yourself! This is
wonderful—you are so talented...and today
is our twenty-seventh wedding anniversary.
What a perfect present.

From bride Karli Gray:

> So cute! Perfectly encapsulated us!

From bride Elise Nikolaisen:

> *Jenny!!!!!!!* This is *so* incredible. I have tears in my eyes!!!!! Thank you so, so, so much for choosing *us* as the couple for the Vows section. We are so grateful and can't wait to amplify this *everywhere!* You're a gem. This means more to us than you know! We appreciate the time you spent with us and invested in the story.

And from her groom Bailey Carlin:

> Also just jumping in to say thank you so much. It is such an honor and privilege to have our love story told so beautifully by you. Thank you *so* much.

From groom Jack Seemer:

> It turned out so good! Thank you, Jenny, for taking your time to get to know us and tell our story. So many friends have reached out already to let us know how much it touched them.

From Amazon reviews of my book; Be That Unicorn:

This is a joyous read! It is relatable and instantly useful. Stop being your worst critic and start living the authentic you. Find it, embrace it, share it. The world is a better place when you can be that unicorn. Love the message and the clever set-up of the book. Great read!

What a perfect read for times like these. Jenny's light shines through every page. An uplifting bundle of wisdom, the entire world could use. Love it!

Loving everything about this book. It's cute and compact—easy to throw in your bag to take anywhere. The author is very engaging and endearing. It's great how she explores different sides to things in a clever and relatable manner. Her thoughts on [topics ranging from] planning and being organized to how important it is for us to help others make this a delightful and encouraging read. I would highly recommend this book and am keeping it close to refer back to certain chapters for a shot of confidence and encouragement anytime.

It's really nice to be able to read these back and feel the love, especially when I'm feeling low. It's so much easier to manifest when you feel happy and strong. But sometimes when we need to manifest the most is when we are not really feeling either of those things. So, reading from your compliment box can help you get into the right mindset to really get your badass manifesting in gear.

And badasses know that we can attend to our own complaint boxes too—the complaints we put in ourselves, of course. We must choose to leave the rest unaddressed. If it's not our circus, then they're not our monkeys...

Here are a few of my complaints to myself, including how I addressed them.

I talk too much.

Response: No one has ever actually said that to me or to anyone else that I am aware of. To the contrary, people often say how easy I am to talk to and how much they enjoy talking to me.

I procrastinate too much.

Response: I always get things done in the end. I actually work well under pressure. I do a good job, and I do it in natural time. Creative work is a different animal. I can't always write. Ideas don't always come. Sometimes I'm just not feeling it, and that's okay. I get the writing done.

I don't proofread well enough.

Response: I have never received this complaint. I am very careful. Mistakes happen. The brain plays tricks when you are reading the same thing over and over. No one is perfect. I am not perfect. I do my best.

I'm a bad mom.

Response: My daughter is amazing. She is happy and self-sufficient and smart and funny and kind. All of that is because of me, not in spite of me. I am not the perfect mom. There is no such thing. I am the most well-intentioned mom, and I do my best in every way I can.

I'm a bad dog mom.

Response: My puppies past and present love me. I take excellent care of them. It's okay to travel. I always leave them in the best hands. I can't always sit on the couch and pet them, although sometimes I wish I could.

I don't volunteer enough.

Response: I do a lot. I do as much as I can. Anything is better than nothing. And if I want to do more, I can. That is up to me. There is no one judging me but me.

That last bit of that last response is important. People are complimenting you all of the time. They are rarely judging you.

It's just that it's so much easier to hang on to the complaints rather than the compliments. So I challenge you to flip the script: let the compliments wash over you and fill you up, and allow the complaints to just slither away into nothingness where they belong.

That can actually be a great manifesting visualization exercise. Imagine a compliment as a flower crown, a silken cape, or a wash of glitter. Imagine it filling you with joy, pride, and happiness. Now, imagine a judgment or a complaint. Form it into a snake in your mind and watch it slither off. It's not your problem. Let it zip away into nowhere. It's not serving you. It doesn't deserve a place with you.

And the truth is, so much of the hate we receive isn't even about us, it's about the hater. I remember the first time I ever got a true piece of hate mail. It was from someone who'd read my first book. It was an email filled with anger and violence. As I read it, I got hot and my stomach turned. I called my dad.

"Read it to me," he said. "No," I told him. "Read it to me," he insisted. "I'll forward it to you," I offered through tears. "No," he emphasized. "You need to read it to me." Somehow I did, as I wiped my nose and stifled my tears. And the more I read, the more I understood. "This isn't about me," I said to my dad.

"Nope," he said. "Not a word of it. The book made him look inward, and he did not like what he saw."

I'd been ready to take a boat to Goona Goona and never look back—as Papa used to say—and yet this guy wasn't even talking about me. He was just directing his own self-loathing at me. It was one of the most important realizations in my life. As I mentioned earlier, my dad always says, and always in the nicest possible way, "No one cares about you."

Remember, he isn't talking about those close to me who love me. He's talking about strangers. They don't know me. How can they love or hate me? All they know is what I bring up for them, and that's about them, not me. So, there's no reason for me to allow their words to affect me at all, let alone take me down.

Let the love wash over you. Let the hate swirl down the drain. You are amazing. Hear that: *You are amazing!*

You are a badass.

You can take a compliment and you can reply to your own complaint box.

I am a badass.

I can take a compliment, and I can reply to my own complaint box.

Manifesting Moments

"To me, manifesting is about setting intentions for what you want to achieve. It's about putting your mental and physical energy into obtaining a goal. If you think it and believe it, you can (and typically will) achieve it.

An element of manifesting that's key to success is letting everyone and everything around you know your intentions, because it cannot be done in a silo. Surrounding yourself with others who share supportive positive energy toward your intention will almost always equal successful manifestations.

For me, the word evokes hope, possibility, and commitment. You have to remain positive and focused on your intention. I've manifested many things in my life!

According to my mom, when I was a kid, I made a list of the things I wanted in life: to own a BMW (I was like twelve years old), be in a fraternity, and live and work in a major city—and I've achieved every one of them.

Our wedding was even a manifestation. We knew we wanted something different; I made a mood board, created a presentation deck, and shared the concept with everyone we knew...and slowly it came together.

This year, we made a vision board (a very literal tool for manifesting), and so far, I've been successful at making the board come to fruition. We see it every day, we show it to people, and we remind one another of our goals, and because of it, we've achieved our vision."

—Jamon Deaver, VIBE Manager

"To me, manifesting is the work to reverse engineer a desired outcome. It's the planning, execution, and sometimes the recalibration of the plan when something goes wrong. Manifesting is the work we put into achieving a goal. Sometimes that work also includes getting over failure and keeping an eye on the prize."

—Margarita Frinsco, Senior Director of Advancement

"Manifesting is the magical art of putting what you want out into the universe and having it come to fruition. I have manifested thousands of things that I know of, both big and small. I've manifested everything from jobs, houses, and relationships down to parking spots. I believe that manifestation is possible all day, every day, if we choose to put our energy toward it and believe in its power."

—Abra Wise, founder of Fern Fest

CHAPTER FIFTEEN

YOU KNOW YOUR STORY AND YOU CAN TRUST WHAT IT TEACHES YOU

If You Can Keep Looking Within, You'll Never Feel Without

You will never feel hopeless, lost, or alone if you look inwards instead of outwards. To look at social media, you would think everyone was rich, hot, wildly successful, and in love. But that's not true, and you know it's not true. We don't know their stories and they don't know ours. You know your truth. You know what's real. You know what you can do. Now's the time to trust your story.

I am a badass.

I know that the only story I can truly know is my own.

What makes me feel badass today?

I am a badass.

I know that the only story I can truly know is my own.

What fear will I face today?

I am a badass.

I know that the only story I can truly know is my own.

What can I do today to make me feel even more badass?

I am a badass.

I know that the only story I can truly know is my own.

What fellow badass can I connect with today?

I am a badass.

I know that the only story I can truly know is my own.

Why is being a badass important to me?

I am a badass.

I know that the only story I can truly know is my own.

They say comparison is the thief of joy. I could not agree more.

I have long been at war with the green-eyed monster. When I was a kid, I was jealous of the girls who got to play Annie, Dorothy, and Audrey in the school plays, while I was always cast as Mrs. Hannigan, the Cowardly Lion, and Audrey II (the plant). As I got older, I became jealous of the popular girls at school. As an adult, I struggle with being jealous of other writers with bigger bylines, more followers, or mailboxes full of goodies from couture lines. I long for approval and attention from the big dogs. The thing is, I'm not really sure why.

I mean I'm human, there's that. But I feel like the Little Mermaid: "I've got gadgets and gizmos a-plenty. I've got whozits and whatzits galore. You want thingamabobs? I've got twenty! But who cares? No big deal. I want more."

The Little Mermaid was jealous of the people walking around on—what do you call them?—feet. But this was only because at that point, she hadn't realized that not only did she already have it all, but the price she would pay for what she thought she wanted wouldn't be worth it—not by a long shot.

I have friends and colleagues who are influencers, and it's a tough row to hoe. They are rarely really enjoying The Thing; they are always trying to *look* like they are enjoying The Thing. Now, don't get me wrong, I'd love to go to the Met Gala. I mean, I'd do almost anything to go to the Met Gala. But I want to really experience it—I don't want to be there and not really *be there.*

So, although I am envious, I am not actually envious of the whole package. That is, I don't want to have to beg public relations folks for access; I don't want to be stuck in standing room only; and I don't want to just be in the room where it happened, I want to be a true part of what's happening. I want to be invited to the Met Gala and to whatever else because they want me—not just a random warm body, and not just someone who can do something for them—to be there. And that, my friend, is the trick to putting on your badass armor and fighting that green-eyed monster. It's along the same lines as, "Be careful what you wish for, because you just might get it."

When I was a kid, I was super jealous of my cousins; we'll call them "Naomi" and "Talia." They were so pretty and fun and sweet, and their parents adored them. Their mother, let's call her my "Aunt Elizabeth," just seemed so thrilled with whatever they did. She was always telling them how beautiful they were, how gorgeous they looked in whatever they wore, and how wonderfully they did, well, everything.

My parents were a good bit more realistic, offering advice about studying more or on choosing clothes that were a bit more flattering, or suggesting a good hair brushing. I wanted Aunt Elizabeth to be my mother. I didn't want to be told to study more, watch less TV, or stay away from culottes.

But here's what I didn't know until many, many years later, Naomi and Talia found their mother quite challenging. She was so sugary sweet that coming to her with anything difficult was really, really difficult. If they said they were sad, angry, or frustrated, the answers were always the same.

"Don't be silly, darling. You look perfect." "Don't be silly, darling. You're too smart to fail." "Don't be silly, darling. Everyone loves you."

The thing was, it's impossible to trust someone to tell you the truth when the sugary sweet coating is so thick that it's impenetrable. Aunt Elizabeth meant well for sure. But what she didn't know is that her over-the-top positivity left her girls always wondering if what their mother was saying was actually true or if it was just overly kind. What a child needs from a parent is honesty, delivered delicately when necessary.

Once I learned the truth about how much Naomi and Talia adored my father, who can sometimes use some work with his delivery but is always spot on with his honesty, I opened my eyes a bit to how one never really knows the whole scoop. Being jealous is not only often based on a false premise, but also frequently serves no purpose.

I mean, admiring someone and working hard to emulate certain traits or achieve certain accomplishments is great. But blind jealousy, that's not so great. The truth is the only person's story we can truly know is our own—and most of us are still constantly working on fully knowing that.

We would be much better served learning more about ourselves, rather than becoming jealous or even defining ourselves and our ability to manifest what we want by looking at others. You are a badass, and you are capable of badass manifesting regardless of the badassery of others.

This applies when it comes to your partner too. You are not your partner. Maybe they have manifested everything they want. Great! Maybe they haven't. Maybe they don't even "believe in all of that manifesting stuff." The thing is, it doesn't matter, because you are you—you are not your partner. In fact, you are not your "lack" of partner, either.

Maybe flying solo is your gig. Maybe you just haven't met the right human.

We live in a very "coupled up" world. Tables are for two. Cruises and other travel arrangements often charge a "single supplement" if you are going on your own and don't opt to be simply paired with someone. But not everyone is partnered.

And regardless, who you are with or whether you presently have a partner does not in any way—or should not in any way—affect your badassery or your badass manifesting abilities.

In fact, some people who are partnered might not feel like a badass in their partner's eye (or in their shadow). Although I respect and understand that feeling, it is one I would love to alleviate for you. If your partner is awesome, you can be awesome too! And if they haven't reached what they define as their "awesome," that in no way means you haven't, can't, or won't.

No matter how well you know your partner, you don't know their journey. And you don't—and can't and won't—ever know them as wholly and completely as you know yourself. So detach your ability to be a badass and manifest in an all-out badass way from theirs. It's separate. You're separate. Even if you're together, you are separate.

This goes double for your family. You are not your parents or your siblings, nor, as I mentioned above,

your cousins. You don't really know them, and
worrying yourself with what you think you know
about their story is simply not helpful.

My dad is a badass. He loves what he loves. He
listens to his gut. He does what he believes despite
people questioning him.

Instead of wishing I was my cousins or that I had
their mom, or at the very least, wishing I had their
relationship with their mom, not only never did
me any good, it was also built on a false premise
that their relationship was perfect and it was the
relationship they wanted and needed.

Turns out, their relationship wasn't any of
those things.

Letting go of comparisons and jealousy can free up
your body, mind, and spirit and give you the mental
space to do the kind of badass manifesting that you
and your life deserve. It also can be a tough thing
to do, but exploring why you feel that way and
what you can do with those feelings instead can
really help.

Begin by asking yourself why. When you are feeling
jealous or find yourself playing the comparing game,
ask yourself why and challenge your answer. Do
you wish you had the job they have? Why don't

you? Do you really want it? Have you tried to get it? Are you qualified for it? If you really want it, what could you do to get it? Are you jealous they have it or just wondering why they have a job like that and you don't?

Then, imagine how you could instead use those feelings in a positive way. What could you do to have the thing they have that you want? What have you done to work against having or getting it yourself? Why? Can you change that? Do you actually want their job, for example, or just their accolades? Or money? Or other status markers?

Use the toddler method. Keep asking "why?" until you land on an answer that is satisfying. Then, keep asking "why not?" until you land on an answer with which you are satisfied. Manifesting what you want is about exploring who you are, how you operate, and what your badass dreams really are, as opposed to what they appear to be.

Comparison is the thief of joy, because we are not them and they are not us.

No one else is you. And that means that you can be whoever you want and manifest the love, life, work, partnerships, friendships, and travel you want. It's perfectly fine to look at other people's lives and

think about what inspiration you can glean from
them in order to create yours.

This:

That job looks interesting.

I might like to live by the water.

One day, I think I would be happy with a partner
like that.

Not this:

I wish I had her job.

I wish I had her house.

I wish I had her partner.

Do you hear/feel the difference? One honors what
the other person has and helps you to find what
you want. The other just feels defeatist, mean, or
sad. It can only make you feel bad. And why do that
to yourself?

Quit the comparison game. Jilt the jealousy project.
We don't even know the truth of those people's
lives. We might well be envying something about
them we would never, ever want.

The only thing I do know about you is this:

You are a badass.

You know that the only story you can truly know is your own.

So say it with me now!

I am a badass.

I know the only story I can truly know is my own.

That's right! And it's an amazing one!

Manifesting Moments

"Manifest to me means to show something through actions, but also to sum up inner feelings or strength to bring something to fruition. I manifested my inner strength when I was undergoing cancer treatment many years ago."

—Gabby McNamara, owner, GMAC Communications

"I was about six or seven years old and wanted a bike. Our family had only been in the United States for two years, and we didn't have a lot of money. We shopped at a grocery store called Auchan's in Houston. They were holding a jump rope contest, and the winner would get a new bike. I wanted to compete for the bike and my parents let me. I visualized winning and saw myself as having the bike, I felt with all my feelings and being that I'd won and that I would come home with a bike that day.

The naivete of a child as well as the sense of wonder of a strong imagination really helped me. I won the contest. I was the last jump roper still jumping and won the bike. I know that may seem silly, but it was huge for me at that age. Since then, various other experiences of knowing and attracting have occurred, but that's always one that I fall back on because having a child's beliefs and naivete really help us avoid doubt. Doubt (even micro doubting) precludes manifestation."

—Elaheh Ashtari, PsyD

"Manifesting, to me, is dreaming your reality into being. I live in the foothills of the Rocky Mountains in a farmhouse on five acres thanks to the divine power of manifestation. I was living in New York City at the time and felt a pull toward the vastness of the mountains, a place that seemed to me to hold more space, and I was desperate to leave apartment life behind. I began to visualize myself walking among the pines and strolling along the creeks. I made a vision board with different images depicting what my new life would look like. I created a morning mantra about living in a house with land near the mountains. Six months later, an acquaintance posted on Facebook that she was breaking her lease to move for a teaching job, and with one phone call, the house was mine—outdoor bathtub and all."

—Christina Cherry, writer

"I've manifested so much in my life—both good and bad. For me, it's about subconsciously directing what you want and need, then guiding yourself into the right spaces to make it happen. For example, I had a vision of the kind of house I wanted, and through an incredibly unlikely scenario, I found it and was able to buy it at a price I could afford. The same thing has happened with landing dream jobs. I haven't hit the lottery jackpot yet, but I do win small amounts regularly—proof, I think, that the universe has a sense of humor."

—Kati Murphy, bon vivant

"To manifest is to dream with your inner knowing—speak, think, will something into existence."

—Diana Kordek, Registered Nurse

"I used to live in fear of wanting too much, shrinking my dreams before life could disappoint me. Manifestation helped me unlearn that. I stopped rehearsing worst-case scenarios and started retraining my brain to expect better. That's not magic—it's neuroscience. When you believe you're worthy, your mind starts filtering the world through possibility instead of fear."

— Mandy Ansari

CONCLUSION

~~~

YOU DON'T JUST HAVE THE MAGIC, YOU ARE THE MAGIC. NOW LET'S MAKE SOME MAGIC!

Manifesting is magical, but it isn't magic. It's really what you make of it, you know. My dad always says, "You may not hit a home run every time you go up to bat. But you definitely won't hit one if you don't at least take a swing."

The mechanics are simple—

Write it down.

Say it in your head.

Say it out loud to yourself.

Share it with someone else.

Envision how it feels to have it become a reality.

Envision sharing that reality with someone.

Live as if it's already real.

Make the calls. Send the emails. Create the connections. Push yourself into the world where you want to be. Take the necessary steps. This isn't a "good things come to those who wait on the couch" kind of thing. This is a "universe helps those who help themselves make things happen" kind of thing.

This is a process, and I hope it will be a fun one. It won't always be easy. Sometimes it might even get scary. But you have all the tools you need. Now's the time to leap!

Trust yourself, trust the universe, and go for it!

You just might surprise yourself. And the universe just might surprise you...

I would love to keep in touch and hear all about your journey! Please find me on Facebook, Instagram, and TikTok @ TheJennyBlock. Or leave me a note at www.badassmanifesting.com.

And I would be so appreciative if you'd leave a review online at Amazon or wherever you purchased the book—or any place reviews are allowed. I hope you will love this book and this journey so much that you'll share it as your favorite gift to give too. It's all the more fun to do this with others, so don't be afraid to share your journey.

Let's go, badasses! There is much badassary manifesting to be done!

Story Storage

Every story you have to tell is important in some way. Sometimes we discover almost in real time why that story is important in our lives. Other times, it might take days, weeks, or years to fully see its significance. But every one of our stories informs our lives, from the simplest lessons to the most grand ones.

Storing our stories and revisiting them can really help us to hone in on what we can (or did or could) learn from them. Sometimes we can even find more or deeper meaning in our stories by returning to them. Sometimes they are simply comforting. Other times, they remind us of what we have accomplished or overcome, which can be incredibly reassuring.

Here are some story starters to help you to remember stories that you might want to store here.

A time when you felt you achieved the impossible.

A time when you helped someone in need.

A time when you faced a dramatic change.

A time when you fell ill.

A time when you lost someone.

A time when you changed someone's life.

A time when you gave more than you thought you had to give.

A time when you thought you were lost but actually found yourself.

A time when you realized that the universe really is on your side.

Keep a record of your stories. They will remind you what a badass you really are. You are your stories, and your stories are badass.

Mantra Manufacturing

We are always learning and experiencing new things. We are always building new pathways in our brains by talking to people, as well as by seeing, doing, laughing, playing, and finding out all the things we never knew that we never knew.

Each experience can help us to create a new mantra. Let's say you see someone giving a salesperson a hard time. You might think to yourself, "Why is she being so awful to her?" But you also want to think, "What is going on in that person's life that she felt compelled to behave that way?"

Is she an awful person? Maybe. Or maybe today was just a terrible day for her. Maybe her cat is sick or she lost her job or her bestie isn't speaking to her. None of those excuse her behavior. But they all absolutely explain her behavior.

And what about the salesperson? Was she in the wrong? Did the issue have anything to do with her at all? Is it reasonable that the customer is upset even if the customer is not sharing her needs in a productive way?

Here's where mantra manufacturing comes in! Here are a few ideas—

I'm a badass.

I know when to take responsibility for my mistakes.

I'm a badass.

I know when not to take things personally.

I'm a badass.

I know not to take out my feelings on other people.

I'm a badass.

I know that it's okay to ask to have my needs met, but I have to do it kindly.

Think none of that has anything to do with manifesting a badass life? Think again. Taking responsibility for your mistakes, asking in kind ways to have your needs met, not taking things personally, and refraining from taking out your feelings on other people are all part of living like a true badass. When you live your life in this way, you are being your badass self—that is, your higher self. And when you do that, good things will come.

Trust me, even if it looks like the Karens get their way, in the end, they get what's coming to them. And you don't want any part of that.

Takeaway Treasure Chest

I love this spot. It's where the good stuff lives. When you read something in this book, or anywhere else for that matter, that feels like a nugget that can serve you, tuck it away here. Maybe you heard something in a movie, at a lecture, or during a conversation with a friend.

Having a takeaway treasure chest is an amazing resource. When you need to fill up your badass cup, you can look back into your chest to find the nugget you need. There's a misnomer that being a badass means you don't need any external support, information, or inspiration. But that simply isn't true.

The secret of every badass is that a badness knows where to seek what she needs, whatever that need might be. What you are seeking is almost always a call, an email, or a Google search away. Here is the place to store those goodies that you may want to revisit. Mine is filled with quotes, links, and books, and even movies and photos.

Reminding myself of amazing past accomplishments—both mine and others'—can really help to get me out of a rut when I'm stuck in one. And sometimes, just knowing that it's there is all I need. I can jump in to a project, a job, or an adventure comfortable in the knowledge that if I get stuck or scared, the help I need is just a breath away.

Think of your takeaway treasure chest like
Dumbo's feather: You can fly without it for sure.
But you don't have to.

Compliment Cabinet

This is where the words that fill your inner cup should be kept and treasured. It can be all too easy to get lost in the bad stuff. And somehow, it seems like one even slightly negative word can make us forget all of the amazing positive things that we are told.

I know I am terribly guilty of this; one negative word and I'm in a tailspin. Heck, one sideways glance and I am gone. Yet, half the time—at least—that word or glance doesn't have a thing in the world to do with me!

Keeping a compliment cabinet really helps. It gives me a place to look back and be reminded of all of the people whose lives I have touched, whose days I have made, or whose worlds I have brightened, even just a little.

So, use this space. Jot down reminders, fill it with sticky notes, or glue in an envelope—whatever works for you. Just save those compliments. Save them up and use them. Take in those words. Soak them up. Every single one is a validation of what a badass you are and of all the badass things you have done and have yet to do!

Complaint Compartment

Here's where the complaints go. You can write your complaints about yourself, your life, your choices, your day. And then you can choose how to address them—including simply letting them go. You can also use this as a spot to jot down and release other people's complaints.

Now, since it's your life, those complaints are not necessarily your problem. You can use the processing pages to work out how or if you want to resolve those. Sometimes, just writing them down is enough to allow you to release them and not waste any more energy on them.

Remember, often people's complaints have nothing to do with you and everything to do with them. Keep in mind the story I shared in Chapter 14 about the very first time I got a piece of hate mail; I was shaking. I got hot all over. My eyes filled with tears, and I felt like I was going to be sick. I called my dad, as I often do when I feel like my world is falling apart. He asked me to read it aloud to him. And when I did, I was actually able to hear what those words were really saying. They had nothing to do with me. They were froma person who was hurting. And they were directed to the people who hurt that person. It's crucial to compartmentalize your complaints. There's no better method when it comes to releasing their power over you.

_____

_____

_____

_____

_____

_____

_____

_____

_____

_____

_____

_____

_____

_____

_____

_____

_____

_____

_____

_____

Processing Pages

Here's a great place to jot down your thoughts—positive and negative—about your badass manifesting journey. If you're trying to wrap your head around a story's takeaway or a takeaway's mantra or to figure out how to resolve a complaint you have about yourself, this is a great place to make doodles, notes, and lists—or perhaps do some freewriting—to figure out where you are.

I tend to spin and let my mind meander all over the place, and all too often, it doesn't lead me anywhere useful. Using my processing pages allows me to work out whatever is spinning in my head. It's amazing how getting something down in writing can help you to figure it out or even simply release it.

Sometimes processing is not about solving a conundrum but rather about setting yourself free. It can also help you discover spots in your life that you may want to dig deeper into, things you might want to work through with a friend or counselor, or ideas you might want to look into further.

In the musical *Wicked*, Fiero sings about the "unexamined life." "Life is fraught-less / When you're thoughtless." It's funny in the show, but funny sad—because it's both true and not true. Sure, you can just act like everything's fine and you don't have a care in the world. But even a badass has bad days. Even a badass faces challenges. Even a badass hits a wall or two. Pretending otherwise if just that—pretending.

It might feel good in the moment to believe you can just move through the world by "dancing through life." But the truth is, living inauthentically is no fun. And until we face our dragons, we can't ever manifest the best for ourselves.

So, do your processing. Take the time. Untangle the knots.

Manifest your badass self by figuring out just exactly who that person is.

Note: Freewriting is just what it sounds like. You write out whatever is on your mind. It doesn't have to make sense—not even to you! You can write down words or phrases, thoughts, or lists. You just write until your brain feels done.

ACKNOWLEDGMENTS

I hardly know where to start when it comes to who to thank. I want to thank Brenda Knight, who manifested this book into a reality with me. I want to thank my wife, who never seems to think any of my writing dreams are crazy—even the crazy ones. I want to thank my dad, who has been pointing me in the right direction, holding me up, and never letting me give up even when I really, really wanted to.

I want to thank my daughter for always telling me the truth even when I don't necessarily want to hear it. Thank you to my BFF, Rachel Pinn, who edited this book, listens to all of my wild ideas, and supports anything and everything I do no matter what, seriously—No. Matter. What. Thank you to my Festie Bestie, who is the best cheerleader a girl could wish for.

And thank you to the entire team at Books That Save Lives for all of their hard work bringing this book to life!

Thank you to all of the badasses in my life and to all of the badasses in the world and throughout history. Your badass lives made my badass life possible.

Last but not least, thank you to my dogs, Walter, who slept through it all, and sadly passed away just 6 months before this book was released, and Aurora, who reminded me every writing day when it was time to get up to walk!

ABOUT THE AUTHOR

Jenny Block is a Lambda Literary Award–winning author, writer, and speaker.

She and her last book, *Be That Unicorn: Find Your Magic, Live Your Truth, and Share Your Shine*, have been featured in and on a variety of websites, publications, podcasts, and TV shows, including *Dallas Voice*, *Drag Star Diva*, *Grit and Grace*, *Great Day Houston*, *So Booking Cool*, *AM Northwest*, *Canvas Rebel*, *Voyage Houston*, and many more.

Jenny is a frequent contributor to the *New York Times*, and, in addition to *Be That Unicorn*, she is also the author of *The Ultimate Guide to Solo Sex*; *O Wow: Discovering Your Ultimate Orgasm*; and *Open: Love, Sex, and Life in an Open Marriage* (winner of a 2008 Lambda Literary Award).

Having written for HuffPost for many years, she has appeared regularly on HuffPost Live and the *HuffPo Sex and Love Podcast*, and is featured in HuffPo's first ever free-standing multimedia project.

She holds both her BA and her MA in English from Virginia Commonwealth University and taught college composition for nearly ten years.

Her work has appeared in and on a wide variety
of publications and websites, including MSNBC,
FoxNews.com, Swaay.com, CuratedTexan.com,
Yahoo Travel, Playboy.com, TheDailyMeal.com,
Jezebel.com, YourTango.com, American Way, the
Dallas Morning News, the *Dallas Voice*, EdgeDallas.
com, and *Curve Magazine*.

She has been featured as an expert on women's
issues, travel, and lifestyle topics for *Brides*
magazine, Cosmopolitan.com, Romper.com,
YourTango.com, Bustle.com, *Woman's Day*
magazine, SheKnows.com, and many others.

Jenny has appeared on a variety of TV and radio
programs, including *Nightline*, *Fox and Friends*,
The Glenn Beck Show, *The Tyra Banks Show*, *Good
Morning Texas*, *The Morning Show with Mike and
Juliet*, FoxNews.com, Playboy Radio, *The Alan
Colmes Show*, *The Young Turks*, and BBC Radio.

A variety of publications and sites have written
about or reviewed her books, including *Playboy*,
YourTango.com, *Publishers Weekly*, *Library Journal*,
Glamour, *Marie Claire*, *Curve*, *Observer* (UK), *Maxi*
(Germany), *Cosmopolitan* (Germany), *Psychologies*
(UK), *Playgirl*, NPR's *Morning Edition*, the *New York
Times*, Feministing.com, the *San Francisco Chronicle*,
the *New York Daily News*, *2: The Magazine for*

Couples (Canada), WomenOnWriting.com, and the *Baltimore City Paper*.

Jenny has also spoken in bookstores and at events all across the country, including at the Catalyst Convention, Brain Tease Dallas, the Wyly Theatre, the Texas Theater, Georgetown University, and the Science Museum of Virginia. She has also performed on Olivia Travel charters on Holland America Cruises, as well as at Michigan Fern Fest, the Patio Pub, Big Mouth Girl and Olivia Travel take-overs at Club Med.

Books That Save Lives came into being in 2024 when the editor and publisher, Brenda Knight, heard directly from readers and authors that certain self-help, grief, psychology books, and journals were providing a lifeline for folks. We live in a stressful world where it is increasingly difficult not to feel overwhelmed, worried, depressed, and downright scared. We intend to offer support for the vulnerable, including people struggling with mental wellness and physical illness as well as people of color, queer and trans adults and teens, immigrants and anyone who needs encouragement and inspiration.

From first responders, military veterans, and retirees to LGBTQ+ teens and to those experiencing the shock of bereavement and loss, our books have saved lives. To us, there is no higher calling.

We would love to hear from you! Our readers are our most important resource; we value your input, suggestions, and ideas.

Please stay in touch with us and follow us at:
www.booksthatsavelives.net
https://www.instagram.com/booksthatsavelives/

www.ingramcontent.com/pod-product-compliance
Lightning Source LLC
Jackson TN
JSHW021119090925
90097JS00001B/1